Making Transitions Work
Navigating the Changes

*E. Lisbeth Donaldson
Bryan Hiebert, Michael Pyryt,
Nancy Arthur*

Detselig Enterprises Ltd.

Calgary, Alberta, Canada

1998

Making Transitions Work
© 1998 Detselig Enterprises Ltd.

Canadian Cataloguing in Publication Data

Making transitions work

Includes bibliographic references.
ISBN 1-55059-168-1

1. School-to-work transition. I. Donaldson, E. Lisbeth (Ethel Lisbeth)
LC1037.M34 1998   370.11'3   C98-910107-X

Detselig Enterprises Ltd.
210-1220 Kensington Rd. N.W.
Calgary, Alberta T2N 3P5
Phone: (403) 283-0900/Fax: (403) 283-6947
e-mail: temeron@telusplanet.net

Detselig Enterprises Ltd. appreciates the financial support for our 1998 publishing program, provided by Canadian Heritage and other sources.

All rights reserved. No part of this book may be reproduced in any form or by any means without permission in writing from the publisher.

Printed in Canada

ISBN 1-55059-168-1

SAN 115-0324

Cover design by Ken Richardson

Table of Contents

Preface v
A Note to the Reader: The Permanent Cat vii

Chapter 1:
The Context of Change for Today's Youth
– *Hiebert, Donaldson, Pyryt, Arthur* 13

Chapter 2:
Managing Cross-Cultural Transitions – *Arthur* 35

Chapter 3:
Skills for Navigating Life Transitions – *Hiebert* 63

Chapter 4:
Matches and Mismatches in Student and Employer Perceptions – *Donaldson* 93

Chapter 5:
Career Development and Self-Development:
Features, Challenges, Resources – *Pyryt* 121

Chapter 6:
Anticipating Milestone Transitions
– *Pyryt, Hiebert* 137

Chapter 7:
Navigating Transitions Well: Success Stories
– *Donaldson, Hiebert, Pyryt, Arthur* 155

Chapter 8:
Forecasting: Millenia Transition Trends
– *Arthur, Hiebert, Donaldson, Pyryt* 169

Index 181

Preface

Everyone is familiar with important life transitions but they are difficult to talk about. A transition period is a time of uncertainty, characterized by conflicting emotions and ambiguous goals. It may be painful to experience, even when outcomes indicate success. Although we all know that we must cultivate good health and endure disease and disappointment, suffer bereavements and enjoy achievements, shed student roles and become employed, the process is individualized. No one experiences these transitions in the same way, but all are formative milestones in the life journey.

This book is a guide. Readers will identify with parts of every chapter, perhaps gleaning understandings about how to advise young people or to contextualize their own transitions. The book is aimed at multiple readership: university students and advisors, high school teachers and counselors, parents, employers, youth workers, social workers, career and employment counselors, and service providers working within community agencies. The book has a generalist approach that avoids extensive jargon and encourages interdisciplinary connections. Nevertheless, the authors have drawn extensively from their research, and that of others, so that the discussion is substantive: it summarizes networks of knowledge and identifies some black holes. The focus of this book is upon how 15-30 year old young people might learn to cope better with important transitions. Perhaps the result will be more positive consequences for themselves and for all with an investment in the future.

Respecting accumulated expertise – both personal and professional – the authors wanted to avoid a program and a policy approach to issues. Given the high profile that transition problems have been allotted during the past two decades, the intent is to stimulate discussion about larger contexts that shape the need for programs and policies. It is time to move beyond a crisis perspective, to build paradigms that accept these transitions as normal and to learn how to make them "work" for both individuals and society. Squandering human talents is as wasteful as financial mismanagement. However, most individuals prefer self-governance to imposed controls. Between the two poles of *laissez-faire* democracy and dictatorship, professionals attempt to help other people successfully navigate various types of life transitions. We hope they find this guide useful.

The four authors have themselves worked in various capacities as human resource professionals. As faculty at the University of Calgary, they collaborate in a graduate course about transitions, conduct research about the issues and serve on many relevant committees and associations. They all have presented their work at international and national conferences. And, they derived their interest in the issues from personal experience as well as professional expertise.

Authorship varies by chapter: some content evolved from interdisciplinary collaboration and some is based upon insights derived from patient years of data analysis. Chapter One sketches the context of change for today's youth. In Chapter Two the focus is upon cross cultural transitions, and trends associated with increasing globalization. Chapter Three identifies skills that assist in the navigation of life transitions. Chapter Four is a discussion about school-to-work matches and mismatches. Chapter Five indicates how career and self-development are inextricably linked. Chapter Six is an argument for anticipating milestone transitions. Chapter Seven profiles the stories of people who have experienced successful transitions. Chapter Eight forecasts the future, outlining millennia trends. Key words are indexed and each chapter has selected bibliographies that list other resources. Email addresses and brief biographies have been provided and we will be interested in reader comments. However, before you begin, read our note to you, the reader, about "The Permanent Cat."

As lead author, I acknowledge the others and appreciate the commitment of the publisher. It is a privilege to work with Bryan Hiebert, Michael Pyryt and Nancy Arthur: their intelligence stimulates my own thinking and their collegiality makes work fun. Christine Bourgeois, the graphics and support staff, is both creative and meticulous, plus she is unfailingly cheerful even when we ask for more revisions. At Detselig Enterprises Ltd., Ted Giles and Linda Berry are a first-rate team and a first-choice publishing company of many authors because of their professionalism. Thank you also to the University of Calgary, which provides the intellectual environment which nurtures projects such as this one.

A Note to the Reader

Transition means different things to different people. It is our hope that this book will help you think about transitions from a new perspective and that it will provide you with useful and innovative ways of helping people feel empowered to deal with the transitions they are facing. To that end, we invite you to read and reflect on the chapters in this book and to explore ways of personalizing the concepts. In the final analysis, it is the meaning that you attach to the stories and concepts in this book that will determine the impact of the book in your life and the lives of the people with whom you work.

To begin the process of personalizing the meanings you attach to what you read, we invite you to reflect upon the word "transition." What does the word transition mean to you? What kinds of images does the word "transition" evoke in your mind? Take one minute and jot down all the words that come to your mind in response to the question: "What does the word 'transition' mean to you?" Then, read the following story. The story of Mr. Tibbs has helped numerous people think of career transitions in a new and energizing way. We think it depicts a new way of looking at job transition that is both healthy and empowering.

THE PERMANENT CAT
by Michelle Tocher

There was once a cat by the name of Mr. Tibbs. A very fine cat, indeed. A sleek and grey Siamese. Mr. Tibbs had been a loyal house cat all his life, and was proud of his long service as a mouser.

So you can imagine his surprise when his mistress put him out on the street one day. "I'm sorry, Mr. Tibbs," she said, "but there isn't a mouse in the house anymore, so we haven't a need for you. Thank you for your long service, dear, you've been very sweet." She gave him a recommendation, rolled it into his collar and shut the door.

Poor Mr. Tibbs! He felt downright betrayed. He had been in that house for seven years! All the same, he reminded himself, he was a fine cat, a Siamese, and a very good mouser, indeed. Surely there ought to be others with mice who were interested in a permanent cat. So he went to the house down the street.

He meowed. An old man opened the door. He had white hair and kindly eyes. "Hello," purred Mr. Tibbs. "My name is Mr. Tibbs. I am 7 years old, and I am looking for a permanent home. I am a fine mouser. I am loyal and fully domesticated. In short, I am a permanent cat." He cocked his head to one side, looking very proud.

"I'm sorry," said the old man. "I can't take a permanent cat."

"Don't you have mice?" asked Mr. Tibbs.

"Well, yes, I've got mice, and I'd like to be rid of them too, but like I said, I can't take a permanent cat."

The old man shut the door. Mr. Tibbs walked down the alleyway, confused. He tried another door, and then another. It was the same story. Lots of mice, but no one would take a permanent cat.

Late in the day, while he was pawing through some trash trying to scare up dinner, along came an alley cat. She bounded through the litter, causing every living thing to jump and run. There was dinner all around her. Mr. Tibbs crouched and growled. Who did she think she was, making such a commotion? You would think she had the world by the tail.

She leaped on top of the garbage can above Mr. Tibbs' head. "Well, well, what do we have here?" she purred in a deep voice. "A fine gentleman."

"A permanent cat," said Mr. Tibbs.

She laughed. "A permanent cat?" She jumped off the can. "Well, I suppose I'm a permanent cat too. Permanently independent." She began to saunter off.

"Wait a minute," said Mr. Tibbs following after. "Don't you work? Don't you need strokes like the rest of us?"

"Oh, I need strokes," she said. "I am currently employed by Mr. Beetleham, down on 53rd. But I don't suppose he's going to have mice forever."

"Then what will you do?"

"I'll go someplace else."

"What ever happened to the principle of loyalty?" said Mr. Tibbs, sulking.

The alley cat stopped. She surveyed him. She sidled by him. She walked around him. "What's your name?" she purred.

"Mr. Tibbs," he said, gathering himself up.

"Well Mr. Tibbs, you're a fine cat. I can see that. But if you want to survive you're going to have to take a little walk on the wild side. Let go of all that permanent stuff. Follow me. I'll show you how to make the transition."

So Mr. Tibbs followed the alley cat. After several weeks, he was ready to seek employment once again, and he returned to the old man's house. He had liked the look of the sofa in his living room.

He meowed at the door and the old man opened it. "Hello," purred Mr. Tibbs. "My name is Mr. Tibbs. I understand you have a problem with mice."

"I do indeed," said the old man.

"I see. And do you have any other needs in a cat?"

"Well, I could do with a little companionship. But I'm old, you know. I don't want to worry about a cat if I have to move on."

"Well, sir," said Mr. Tibbs, "I have been a domestic cat for seven years, so I make an excellent companion, and I have the references to prove it. I am also a trained mouser. And because I am completely independent, I will have no trouble surviving if you have to put me back out on the street. I will also return to the street if I am unhappy in your home."

"Oh, you dear cat," said the old man. "I will do my utmost to give you the best home I can." He lifted him up, and took him inside.

So Mr. Tibbs got a special place on the sofa, his favorite food and many strokes. He loved the old man, and his love was permanent, though he never forgot, he wasn't a permanent cat.

© *Michelle Tocher, 1995*

* * *

Take a moment right now and complete again the thought listing task we invited you to do before you read the story. What do you notice? What words are different in the two lists? What themes are different in the two lists? Likely you will notice some differences. If so, it is a reflection of how your thinking has changed in the short time that it took for you to read the story. With similar reflection, the change process in your own experience will continue as you read this book. The thought listing procedure outlined above often helps people become more aware of the impact of the experiences in which they engage.

As you read through this book, we hope you will go beyond the words on the pages and get in touch with the meanings underlying the words. Young people today live in a very different world than did their parents and grandparents. They face different challenges and they require different skills to meet those challenges successfully. The practical, yet theoretically accurate, nature of this book, coupled with your active engagement in the reading process, will help to make sure that your experience with the content in this book will be personally relevant and will translate into your interaction with the young people you work with.

E. Lizbeth Donaldson
Bryan Hiebert
Nancy Arthur
Michael Pyryt

* * *

About the Authors . . .

All four authors may be contacted by mail at: Faculty of Education, University of Calgary, 2500 University Drive N.W., Calgary, AB T2N 1N4.

E. Lisbeth (Betty) Donaldson, Associate Professor, Faculty of Education, University of Calgary, has been conducting research on student transitions for more than ten years. Results have been published in various publications, and she has received several international and and national awards for her work. She is past-president of the Canadian Association for the Study of Women and Education and of the Canadian Recreational Canoeing Association, a recreation that provides experiential learning for life transitions. She teaches graduate courses on transitional issues and women's education. Other research interests include comparative analyses of policies and programs related to serious disruptive behavior in schools. For further information, contact: edonalds@ucalgary.ca.

Bryan Hiebert is a full professor and Chair of the Professional Practice Area in the Department of Educational Psychology at the University of Calgary. Dr. Hiebert has been a school teacher, vice-principal, principal and counsellor, in addition to working in private practice and staff training. For the past 14 years, Dr. Hiebert has been president of the Canadian Career Development Foundation. Under his leadership, the foundation completed CAMCRY (Creation And Mobilization of Counselling Resources for Youth), a 20 million dollar national program development initiative, focusing on creating, field testing and disseminating innovative approaches to career counselling with youth and training programs for youth workers. The scope of the initiative included projects for: young offenders, multicultural youth, young social assistance recipients, young women, high school drop-outs, learning disabled students, normally achieving high school students and other youth in transition. For further information, contact hiebert@ucalgary.ca

Michael C. Pyryt, Ph.D., is Associate Professor of Educational Psychology and Coordinator of Research and Program Evaluation at the University of Calgary. Dr. Pyryt has 19 years' experience as a university-based teacher educator and researcher in gifted education. He has presented papers at national and international conferences and has published papers on topics such as self-concept, learning styles, values, career development issues, teacher and peer perceptions, computers, science programs, acceleration, leadership, and creativity as they relate to gifted individuals and gifted education. For further information, contact mpyryt@ucalgary.ca.

Nancy Arthur is an Assistant Professor in the Department of Educational Psychology at The University of Calgary. As a counsellor educator, Nancy has special interests in career transitions and preparing professionals for working with culturally diverse populations. Nancy has more than 15 years counselling experience in post-secondary education. Prior to joining the faculty at The University of Calgary, she was employed as a counsellor at the Southern Alberta Institute of Technology. Nancy's interest in cross-cultural transitions developed through her roles in international education. Managing international projects, training instructors and coordinating services for international students from more than 20 countries provided the foundation for writing the chapter on making cross-cultural transitions work. For further information, contact narthur@ucalgary.ca.

Michelle Tocher is a writer and storyteller who has been producing educational programs for over 15 years. She has the unique agility to create powerful narratives that can be used by teachers, counsellors and leaders to guide, inspire and promote change. With Masters degrees in the history of science and in journalism, she is author of *The Broad Mind* (an illustrated fable) and *Brave Work: A Guide to the Quest for Meaning in Work*. For further information, contact: mtocher@interlog.com.

Chapter 1
The Context of Change for Today's Youth

*Bryan Hiebert, E. Lisbeth Donaldson,
Michael Pyryt, Nancy Arthur*

Young people today live in a world that is radically different from the one in which their parents grew up. Although many people have had a vague realization of this for some time, most adults and young people are just now beginning to understand the nature of this change and the different types of knowledge, skills and attitudes needed to successfully navigate life's transitions. At the societal level, new technology, globalization of trade and changing population demographics combine to create differences in the pattern of work that most people experience. People are beginning to realize that transition is not a one-time event, but rather a constant state, or at least a recurring state that all people experience. The focus in this book is on youth aged 15 to 30. It may seem like a large age range, but it includes the "official Canadian definition" of youth. In helping these young people plan for successful transitions, it is important to listen to the voices of the people who are involved in their experience. Adults need to listen to young people to determine how to facilitate transition to adulthood in a proactive way. Employers need to listen to workers to find out their experience of the transition process. Today there is a new labor market reality that creates a context for change that is unfamiliar to many, but experienced by everyone. This chapter outlines some of the more important aspects of the current context that need to be considered in order to maximize the chances for successful transitions.

Societal Change

Several trends contribute to the changed and changing context that people face as they attempt to navigate through life circumstances. There is an increased emphasis on technology, both at home and in the work place. Increased globalization means that Canada is not an isolated player in the world economy and is affected by factors over which Canadians have little control. The changing demographics of our country, coupled with the changing nature of work, necessitate a different way of thinking about transitions in general and career transitions in particular. These themes are elaborated below.

Changes In Technology

A brief tour through most homes serves to underscore the impact of technology on today's living. Figure 1 itemizes some technological developments that did not exist 15 years ago, but today are a part of many people's everyday existence.

• VCRs	• internet
• camcorders	• modem computer access
• video games	• cellular telephones
• big screen TV	• global positioning systems
• compact discs	• automobiles with:
• personal computers	anti-lock brakes
• CD-ROM	electronic transmissions
• microwave ovens	air bags
• automated banking	large computer capacity
Figure 1. Common Technological Advances In The Last 15 Years.	

Experts estimate that 70% of Canadians now in the work force will still be in the work force 5 years from now, but that 85% of the technology they will be using has not even been invented yet! (O'Reilly & Alfred, 1995). The need for flexibility, constant re-training and adaptability to new situations is paramount, and will continue to grow.

Globalization

Social and political changes world wide, coupled with increasing globalization, are creating enormous changes in the way people do business. Canada is in a North American Free Trade Agreement with the United States and Mexico and NAFTA faces two major trading blocks, the Pacific Rim and a united Europe. In 1995, the U.S. and Canadian dollars experienced an overnight reduction in purchase value by 15% because the international community distrusted our relationship with Mexico and our interrelation with its weak currency. The value of our dollar on the world economy has since rebounded, but it continues to be somewhat volatile because of Asian monetary crises. These events illustrate how our economy is affected by factors over which we have little control. In the recent past, communism in Russia has given way to a free market economy. Communist China is the fastest growing capitalistic economy in the world. A prominent British bank collapsed because of the trading practices of one man in Singapore. The underlying theme in the above observations is that our economy is affected by decisions in other countries, that hold different values and have different priorities from our own.

Changing Demographics

The composition of Canadian society is changing. The proportion of older people in our population is increasing. The fact that "baby boomers," people born between 1947 and 1966, comprise one-third of our population means that the generations following them face particular challenges. Foot (1996) points out that the front-end boomers have experienced abundant opportunity, stable career paths and relative prosperity. The generations that followed them have encountered very different experiences: high real estate prices, increased competition for diminishing opportunity and a rapidly changing job market. In 1993, the unemployment rate for youth was twice as high as for workers aged 45 years or more. The situation is even worse for youth who leave high school without graduating. In 1995, the unemployment rate was twice as great for high school leavers compared to high school graduates, and three times as high for female high school leavers (Clark, 1997). While the total number of jobs grew by about one-fifth (.20) between 1975 and 1993, the number of part-time jobs increased to more than 2.2 times its 1975 level (Advisory Group on Working Time and the Distribution of Work, 1994). These changes illustrate why the experiences of different generations are so dissimilar, that it is often difficult for adults to understand the experiences of youth. These differences represent more than the fabled generation gap. They are the result of a situation where people's experiences are so different, and the set of circumstances encountered so discrepant, that they have trouble even imagining what the experience is like for the other person.

On the labor scene, there is a similar changing context. The unemployment rate hovers around 9%, however, there is still a shortage of skilled and professional workers. Women entering the labor force comprised about 90% of the labor force growth in the 80s, resulting in the current situation where today women make up about 55% of the work force. About 70% of mothers with children aged 6-17 are working outside the home and 62% of women with younger children are working outside the home or seeking work. In order to fill labor market demands, Canada must turn to immigration. Over the past 10 years, there has been approximately a 250 000 net annual immigration in Canada, or about 1% of our population. The accumulated immigration has changed the composition of many cities. More than one-third of the populations of Toronto and Vancouver are immigrants and Toronto is approaching the 50% mark (Badets, 1993). The effects are also noticed in the composition of most school classrooms across the country.

Putting together the above observations, there are many fronts on which people are facing transitions. Our social structure is undergoing change. Immigrants and other minority groups face special challenges in making their transition into Canadian society (Arthur, 1997; Perron, 1996). Long-time residents face special transition challenges as well in order to adjust to the changing social context. The factors promoting success are very different for handicapped and non-handicapped youth (Chadsey-Rusch, Rusch & O'Reilly, 1996). The transition experiences of female and male adolescents are also very different (Sayer, 1993; Sayer & Ellis, 1986). Combined, these factors underscore the need for continuing flexibility and adaptability on the part of all members of society.

Changing Nature of Work

The composition of the labor force in Canada also is changing. Canada is moving from a resource-based economy to a service-based economy (Hiebert, Jarvis, Bezanson, Ward & Hearn, 1992). Since 1981, 90% of the new jobs created are in the service sector, which now accounts for 70% of all jobs in Canada. Alberta's third largest employer now is telecommunication, passing forestry and industry. It is estimated that by the year 2000, jobs in the information sector will account for 44% of all work. Today, 98% of Canadian businesses have fewer than 100 employees and 75% of all new jobs created are in firms with less than 20 employees. Unskilled jobs are decreasing and the estimate is that by 2000 they will account for only 15% of the labor force. Even in the auto sector, more than 60% of jobs are now skilled or highly skilled. There is an increase in part-time, part-year jobs and an increase in portfolio workers.

People are beginning to understand that the days of working in a large company for life, in a regular full time job, are a thing of the past. Canadian labor mobility data indicate that on the average, Canadians change jobs every 3 years and change occupations every 5 years. Thus, for every worker in a stable job situation (e.g., physicians, school teachers, university professors) there are others who are changing much more frequently in order to produce the averages reported above. This situation has been common knowledge for a long time in the career development community, however, it is now beginning to be understood by the average person in the street.

It is clear to most people now that in order to succeed in today's labor force, people need greater flexibility and adaptability. There are higher expectations for workers and they need a broader range of transferable skills in order to move from one work situation to another. Most analysts agree (O'Reilly & Alfred, 1995) that by the beginning of the 21st century 64% of all jobs will require high school graduation and 50% will require some post-secondary education. However, in spite of this, substantial numbers of youth drop out of high school before they finish. Frank (1996) reports that in 1991, 63% of youth aged 18-20 were high school graduates, 18% had left school without graduating, and the remainder were still in high school. Four years later, about one-quarter of the school leavers had returned to school and completed a high school diploma, bringing the high school completion rate to 85%. However, while programs such as Stay In School (Hackett & Baran, 1995) seem to have been successful in reducing the national rate of high school drop-outs from 30% to a more acceptable level, great regional variations exist. For example, the high school completion rate ranges as low as 75% in Atlantic Canada (Frank, 1996) and hovers around 60% in the North (NWT Education, Culture & Training, 1997). Young men, youth in rural communities and aboriginal youth are particularly over-represented in the school leaver population.

For youth who do remain in school, there is often a bias in favor of academic students bound for college and university. The bias towards post-secondary education is shared by the general populace. Recent surveys in Ontario and Alberta indicate that 78% of grade ten students aspire to college or university and 80% of parents expect their children to attend college or university (Hiebert, Collins & Cairns, 1994). Only 9% of students expect to enter the labor force directly from high school. However, in actual fact, about 32% of students actually finish high school and go on to college or university, while 64% of students actually enter the labor force directly from high school. Furthermore, enrollment caps exist in many college and university programs and entrance requirements are increasing, making it even more difficult to enter a post-secondary program. For those who do enter post-secondary institutions, more than 50% do not complete the program they begin (Hiebert, et al., 1992). In addition, university graduation no longer guarantees a job. Thus, although there is a bias towards post-secondary education in our society, it is unattainable for many young people, and many of those who do attend seem to lack a sense of purpose with their programs of study.

Summary

Wide scale changes in technology, coupled with globalization of trade, changing population demographics and the changing nature of work, have created a context for living that is very different for young people today than it was for their parents. The types of transitions that young people face and the extent of change they experience while making those transitions are of unprecedented proportions. Thus, a different way of thinking about transition is required and different skill sets are needed in order to experience success.

Common Transition Points

Transition is a cyclical repetitive process, enacted across time, and occurring in many domains. People in unique circumstances may face particular types of transitions, however, there are some transition experiences that are shared by sufficiently large numbers of people that they permit a general discussion. Chadsey-Rusch, et al. (1996) identify three types of transitions that most young people face, transitions related to career, independent living and relationships/personal growth.

Career Transitions

Career choices are among the most important choices people make, second only, perhaps, to the choice of mate. Moreover, because people spend about 50% of their waking hours involved in some aspect of their career, and there is substantial carry over between people's jobs and other facets of their lives, career issues tend to become interwoven with all aspects of a person's existence. Most current theorists and practitioners use the term career/life to describe the focus of their work, for it emphasizes that career and life cannot be separated. Using the term career/life underscores the observation that the nature of career has changed over the past 10 years and the components (or dimensions) of career transition are different than they were previously.

Nature of Career

We have devoted a whole chapter to career/life transitions and therefore the concept will only be introduced here, in order to emphasize the importance that career-related concerns have in the minds of most young people. Earlier in this chapter we described the changing nature of the labor force and pointed out that work-related roles are dramatically different for today's youth. Most career development experts (cf. Hoyt, 1988, 1991; Super, 1987; Savickas & Lent, 1997) acknowledge that the concept of career needs to extend beyond paid employment to include a multitude of life roles in which people engage. With this in mind, the following perspective is outlined, not to provide a definitive answer to the question "What is career?", but to encourage readers to begin thinking about the construct of career in a way that is perhaps different from what they considered in the past.

Career is generally thought of as the lifelong practice of managing learning and work (Bezanson & Hopkins, 1998; Hiebert, 1998). Technically speaking, career can only be viewed definitively in retrospect. We look back to chart our career, for it is the sum total of the work and paid employment we have engaged in. However, even though we can only describe our careers retrospectively, we can project a career path into the future. Career/life planning is a meaningful term, because the tools and approaches for career planning are identical to those involved in life planning. However, career and life are not the same. The parts of life that involve play, and routine daily activities such as brushing our teeth, are not part of career. BUT volunteer work, paid employment and sometimes drudgery are all part of career.

Work consists of the things people do that are goal-directed, from which they gain satisfaction and self-fulfillment, and which contribute to larger societal well-being (Hoyt, 1988, 1991). Most often, work is thought of as not tied to paid employment, but to purposeful, meaningful and satisfying activities. For many people, it is volunteer work that keeps their life exciting and provides a sense of personal accomplishment. Work is contrasted with drudgery, which consists of things people do that they don't find fulfilling and/or don't contribute to larger societal goals. Work is also contrasted with play, where an activity might be satisfying, and even self-fulfilling, but doesn't really contribute to larger societal goals and may not have a definite goal (other than to have fun). Whether or not a given activity is work, or play, or drudgery depends a lot on the perspective of the person performing it. Gardening sometimes may be work, sometimes drudgery, sometimes play, even though it may all be called "yard work." However, all of these activities can have a connection with career.

One important implication arising from this way of conceptualizing career is that everyone has a career, even elementary school children. True, their careers have not been very long, but it is nevertheless a career. That is why career education in elementary school makes sense: Not to prepare children for the world of paid employment, but for the future that begins this afternoon and extends forward from there. Recently, Hoyt is advocating eliminating the phrase "transition from school to work" because it implies that school is not work, i.e., that school is not personally rewarding, providing a sense of personal accomplishment, etc. It is important to promote the idea that school is an important part of the career path of youth. For many young people, school is their career and it provides substantial positive contribution to their sense of self. Schooling is not a means to an end, it is a worthwhile pursuit in its own right and part of the developing career/life path of young people. Careers unfold whether or not people plan them. In so doing, a career path may be altered, sometimes quite drastically, but there always are interconnecting threads that can be identified when people look back over their careers. It is these changes in career paths that constitute career transitions.

New Career Development Messages for Youth

The contextual changes described earlier in this chapter suggest a need for a different metaphor to describe career development and a different career development message for young people. Several metaphors provide an appropriate context for career development. One common example is to talk about a career path, in contrast to an occupational destination. Paths usually interconnect with other paths and there often are multiple branching paths. The general direction one is heading may be clear, but the specific place in the forest is not always certain. Trees make another good metaphor for career development. Trees typically have a strong central trunk, but have multiple branches of varying strength and direction. A good root system is necessary for a strong tree, and expert cultivation is necessary, especially when the tree is getting established. When all parts are strong and interconnected, the tree is strong. Any missing ingredient is likely to jeopardize the whole tree. These types of metaphors are more appropriate for helping people understand career in today's world and feel capable of taking a more active part in planning their careers.

A few years ago, a small think tank developed what is becoming a benchmark for the central themes that young people need in order to approach career/life planning in a way that is appropriate for today's world. They have become known as the "High 5" (or High 5 + 1) of career development (Day, Redekopp & Robb, 1994; Redekopp, Day & Robb, 1995) and have great relevance for conceptualizing how to navigate life transitions successfully. They are described briefly below.

Change is constant. We know that the average Canadian changes jobs every 3 years and occupations every 5 years (Hiebert, et al., 1992). Many jobs that exist today will be obsolete in 5 years. Many jobs that will exist 5 years from now do not exist today. It often seems as if the only thing certain is that nothing is certain. Everything is changing, all the time, therefore, it is important to get used to it and to learn to deal with change.

Focus on the journey. Since change is happening so rapidly, the job we are preparing for today may not exist when we have completed our training. Therefore, because the occupational destination is uncertain, it is important to enjoy the journey. The journey is all that can be counted on, so it is important to enjoy it.

Follow your heart. It is a common observation that people tend to strive for, and be motivated by, the things they are interested in. Passion is what drives people's souls. Likely every reader knows people who have made a dramatic change in their mid-40s to pursue a dream that they "always wanted to do." People often feel locked into a program of study or a job that they have little real interest in. Bit by bit, they see their enthusiasm diminishing and the job becomes drudgery. At some point they begin to feel the pull of what they always wanted to pursue. It is important to encourage young people to discover the things that they get excited about and to explore the career options connected with that. How would you have liked to be the counsellor who talked Wayne Gretsky into quitting hockey and pursuing a "real occupation?"

Keep learning. Life long learning is not an option. It happens to everyone, all the time. People do not stagnate, they continue developing – the question is whether or not they want to influence the direction of their development or leave it to chance. It is not a matter of "if" people will keep learning, but of "what" they will continue to learn.

Access your allies. Analysts tell us that 80% of all job hirings are filled as a result of the informal labor market. Personal contacts are the richest source of job leads. Personal networks are what keep our thinking straight (or not), keep us motivated and help us grow. Therefore, it is important to build strong personal networks, keep them strong and access them frequently.

Believe in yourself. After the "High 5" was developed and practitioners began relating the new message to young people, they discovered that there was one overarching part of the message that was missing. Thus, the "High 5 + 1" was born. Belief in self is one of the most important personal characteristics – it pervades everything that people do. If people don't believe in themselves, it will be hard to get others to believe in them. "Believe in yourself" goes beyond the good tummy feeling that many people associate with the term "self-esteem" to incorporate an inner confidence that helps people meet new challenges successfully. It results from exposure to positive role models and engagement with a variety of activities that are approached from a learning perspective. It is important for adults to help create success experiences for young people and to cultivate environments that foster persistence and acknowledge accomplishment. Such an approach will help youth become more aware of their strengths and more able to draw on those strengths to meet the challenges they face. Everyone has many positive characteristics. Feeling successful often is a matter of focusing on the positives, rather than dwelling on the negatives. A positive attitude is an important aspect of career/life planning and one that we need to cultivate in youth.

We live in an exciting and ever changing world. It is easy to feel overwhelmed and unprepared to cope with an uncertain future. However, it is important for us all to focus on the new messages for youth and to help them to build confidence and optimism about the future. Most people realize that career and life are inseparable constructs. The new messages for youth described above really apply to all aspects of peoples' lives, including the other two major transition points described below.

Transitions to Independent Living

Over the past few decades, gaining independence from parents and establishing a self-supporting abode has been considered one of the major indicators of transition from youth to adulthood

(Schaie & Willis, 1986). In years past, this transition was relatively straightforward and predictable. However, increasingly it is becoming more complex and less predictable. It often is delayed for handicapped youth, or youth with other barriers, and increasingly is being delayed for mainstream youth as well. In addition, there is an increase in the prevalence of "boomerang children" who return to their parents' home after a period of trying to make it on their own. The change in living arrangements places additional demands on both parents and youth.

Several factors have been identified as influencing the transition to independent living. Youth from disadvantaged or poor families are less likely to experience successful transitions (Roberts & Parsell, 1992). Children from poorer families are more likely to boomerang home than children of more well-off families (Mitchell & Gee, 1996). People from economically depressed areas have an additional problem, in that children often cannot return home because there are few jobs and often little ability of parents for financial support. Rural students frequently have fewer options available to them than students in urban centres (Lehr & Jeffery, 1996). Aboriginal youth have additional problems in that they leave the important caring figures in their life at a time when they are struggling with cultural identity issues in addition to those pertaining to separation (Gabor, Thibodeau & Manychief, 1996). In a similar vein, international students are more likely to be involved in multiple transition experiences (Arthur, 1997).

Transitions Involving Relationships and Personal Growth

Relational transitions involve courtship and marriage, as well as establishing a social network which can offer support and encouragement in addition to addressing companionship needs. Successful relational transitions require well-developed social skills, which often are taken for granted and seldom taught explicitly. Nevertheless, social skills are important for engaging in successful transitions in all aspects of relationships and personal growth.

Unrau and Krysik (1996) point out that intimacy is a theme underlying many relational transitions. Intimacy refers to close personal relationships that are established throughout life, initially between care-givers and children and later with close friends and intimate partners. However, the sources of intimacy and support tend to be context specific. During adolescence, friends tend to be sought for social support, but parents tend to be sought for input on more consequential decisions. As Lehr and Jeffery (1996) point out, contrary to a widely-held societal myth, young people do consult their parents and value their opinions on important life-impact matters. Later, people tend to develop different sources of social support for the various important life roles in which they engage. People with a network of people in whom they can confide and from whom they can seek input tend to report greater life satisfaction and lower amounts of stress (Hiebert, 1988).

Listening to the Voices of Youth

There is convergence from several difference bodies of literature on the general principle of the importance of understanding the perspective of the central figures involved in an experience. The bulk of the literature on stress and coping emphasizes the importance of understanding a situation as seen through the eyes of the participant in the situation (e.g., Arthur & Hiebert, 1996; Hiebert, 1983, 1988; Lazarus & Folkman, 1984). The literature on teaching and instruction similarly emphasizes the importance of relating to the frame of reference of the learner (e.g., Good & Brophy, 1983; Martin & Martin, 1987). The recent move towards constructivism in the field of counselling and human development (e.g., Peavy, 1992, 1996; Neimeyer, 1993) emphasizes a similar theme. Thus, discussions of youth transition need to attend primarily to the needs of youth as expressed by the young people themselves.

The Importance of Student Self-Reports

Adults often think they know what is best for young people and what sorts of needs young people have. However, research is discovering that there are important discrepancies between the perceptions of adults and the perceptions of students regarding the needs of adolescents. In a recent study of the needs of junior high school students (Hiebert, Kemeny & Kurchak, in press), only two of the students' top 15 needs were in the top 15 list of the school personnel or parents. For 41% of the items, there was no agreement between the student responses and either adult group. Similar differences have been reported in studies of high school students (Collins & Hiebert, 1995; Hiebert, et al., 1994).

Not only are the views of adults different from the views of students, they are often diametrically different. For example, Hiebert, et al. (in press) found that students reported high priority needs in the areas of career planning, the structure of the school day and the school physical plant – these were not identified by either parents or school personnel as being important. Collins and Angen (1997) found that in three high schools, students identified needs pertaining to the school physical plant (such as having doors on washroom cubicles; soap dispensers; removal of grafitti on walls) as being the most important for them, however these were at the bottom, or next to the bottom, of the list for both school personnel and parents. They also found, as did Collins and Hiebert (1995), that sexual and cultural discrimination and harassment, between peers as well as between students and teachers, are seen as important issues by students. These were seen as significantly less important by school personnel and parents. For the most part, school personnel and parents saw emotional problems (e.g., depression, stress), personal problems (e.g., self-esteem, appearance) and interpersonal problems (e.g., relations with family and peers) as paramount needs of adolescents. The student self-reports tended to focus more on finding solutions, rather than reporting problems (e.g., communicating more effectively rather than interpersonal problems). In general, these studies suggest that adults and students have very different views regarding the needs of adolescents.

The above findings suggest that teachers and parents should be cautious about using their perceptions as the basis for developing programs aimed at meeting the needs of youth. If school personnel and parents rely on their own perceptions of what students need, the resulting programs will look very different from those based on student self-reports. The programs based on adult perceptions likely will lack meaning for students. These studies underscore the importance of finding out from adolescents first hand their perceptions of the demands they face, the needs they experience and the types of programming they would find useful to meet those needs.

The Reported Needs of Youth

While it is clear that adolescence is filled with a number of demands, it is also evident that not all adolescents have the same experiences as they move through this transition period (Petersen & Spiga, 1982; Price, 1985; Thoresen & Eagleston, 1983). Thus, any discussion of the needs and demands faced by adolescents should be prefaced with a caution that while some general observations have been made in the literature, important individual differences exist that should be addressed in any comprehensive program. With this caution in mind, it is possible to discuss several observations that have been made by researchers.

One frequent finding in the research literature is that young people tend to be very responsible and the needs they report pertain to finding solutions that will help them deal more effectively with the demands they face. For example, Hiebert & Huston (1992) found that school-related problems topped the list of demands reported by high school students, with 84.7% of their respondents listing at least one school-related situation as one of the top three demands they faced. This was followed by family related concerns (identified by 47.3% of respondents) and part-time jobs (36.3% of respondents). Allen and Hiebert (1991) and Violato and Holden (1988) also found that the most frequently reported concerns of young people were academic in nature. Student workload and stress are prominent concerns in several studies (Allen & Hiebert, 1991; D'Arcy, 1982; Lessard, in press). Several studies also found that students would like to see more attention paid to equity issues and school violence (Collins & Angen, 1997; Collins & Hiebert, 1995; Lessard, in press; Mailandt, in press). In general, the above studies suggest a responsible and solution-focused perspective on the part of young people. The needs they express are related to finding solutions to the problems and concerns they face, rather than a focus on the problems they encounter per se (Collins & Hiebert, 1995).

In numerous investigations, career/life planning concerns are among the highest priority needs reported by adolescents and often the single most important issue youth feel they are facing. For example, in a major national survey of youth, Posterski and Bibby (1988) found that concern about the future was the most frequently identified worry. Even in studies where career-related concerns are not the highest priority, they are frequently in the top group of needs or concerns. For example, Hiebert, et al., (in press) discovered that three of the top five reported needs in their sample pertained to career planning. Collins (1998) reports that the most frequently expressed counselling concern in 5 high schools was career counselling. Similarly, Collins and Hiebert (1995) and Hiebert, et al. (1994) found that career planning needs were consistently among the highest priority needs reported by adolescents. The priority given to career concerns by Canadian young people is similar to their counterparts in the United States. A 1988 American College Testing Program needs assessment of 32 000 high school students revealed that the three highest ranked items were related to career planning and 12 of the top 20 items were career-related. The problem also persists in adulthood. In a 1989 Gallup Poll in the United State, 50% of respondents said that in their present employment, their personal skills, abilities and knowledge were being underutilized. In the same poll, 59% of respondents said they did not have a personal career plan when they began their first full-time job and 65% said if they could plan their work life again they would try to get more information about their career options.

Workload and stress are identified frequently as important areas of concern (Allen & Hiebert, 1991; Collins, 1998; Hiebert & Huston, 1992). These reports seem to represent an accurate assessment by young people of the excessive demands they are facing, for D'Arcy (1982) found that adolescents reported consistently higher symptomatology on the General Health Questionnaire than did an adult sample. Similarly, Allen and Hiebert (1991) found that adolescents demonstrated higher stress and fewer coping resources than adults. Young women report greater stress, more stress symptoms and more intense demands than young men (Allen & Hiebert, 1991; D'Arcy & Siddique, 1984; Holmes & Silverman, 1992). At present, the reason for these differences is not clear. It could be that the pattern of coping exhibited by males more adequately addresses the sorts of demands which male adolescents face. In contrast, it might be that the socialization pattern experienced by females not only creates for them a greater number of demands, but also leaves them poorly prepared to handle the demands they face.

In studies investigating the manner in which adolescents attempt to deal with the demands they face, some startling findings emerge. Generally speaking, young people have meager coping repertoires. For the most part, they have few explicit strategies for dealing with the demands they face, except to work harder, try not to let it bother them or withdraw. Such approaches may be sufficient for dealing with short-term, low-intensity demands, but they are unlikely to be adequate for dealing with persistent, higher intensity demands of the sort that are reported. Current research suggests that peoples' vulnerability to stress is determined by the adequacy of their coping resources. Young people with a wide range of coping options will more likely be able to handle effectively the demands they face. Conversely, young people with deficient coping repertoires will be particularly susceptible to stress, as they will not have the range of coping options to meet the variety of demands they encounter (Allen & Hiebert, 1991; Compas, Malcarne & Fondacaro, 1988; Thoresen & Eagleston, 1983). Such observations lead to the conclusion that the anger and frustration adolescents sometimes experience is not the result of some "stage they are going through," but rather a normal reaction to facing what for them are real and intense demands which they feel unprepared to handle effectively.

Summary

Generally speaking, it is our view that the picture painted above suggests that adolescents are a very responsible group who are concerned about the quality of their school experience, their relationships with family and friends and preparing themselves for making successful transitions into further schooling or employment. The picture represents a dramatic departure from the stereotypical view of adolescence as a period of "storm and stress," fraught with turbulence. These are the type of observations that lead many writers (e.g., Hiebert, et al., in press; Muuss, 1988; Travis & Violato, 1989) to suggest that the picture of adolescence held by many adults, and depicted in the media, represents a distorted perception of the needs, behaviors, and attitudes of adolescents.

Numerous writers (e.g., Allen & Hiebert, 1991; Hiebert, et al., in press; Lessard, in press; Posterski & Bibby, 1988) suggest that adolescents today face a variety of demands for which they generally have been ill-prepared. Young women, aboriginal youth, ethnic minorities and homosexual youth face additional challenges. However, few students receive training in dealing with the sorts of life demands that they face every day. This lack of training means that they are minimally equipped to handle the demands they face on a day-to-day basis, which undoubtedly is a contributing factor to the rising incidence of stress disorders and adolescent suicide (Hiebert, 1991). Researchers believe there is a clear need for program development within schools that will broaden the coping repertoires of adolescents and help them be better prepared to handle the challenges they face (Collins & Hiebert, 1995). The remaining chapters of this book, especially chapters three and four, provide specific suggestions for the types of skills that are particularly needed. As Diachuk, et al. (1995) put it, every school has a clear mandate and responsibility to prepare students for the future by helping them acquire the necessary attitudes, skills and knowledge they need to know and appreciate themselves, relate effectively with others, develop appropriate educational skills and plans, and explore career alternatives.

Conclusion

Transitions are complex processes that are non-linear and last a lifetime. They are mediated experiences, therefore, amenable to influence. Individual and social factors contribute positively and negatively in optimizing transition experiences. Young men and young women in Canadian society have very different experiences (Martin, 1996). Adolescent boys and girls have diametrically different attributions for success and failure (Sayer, 1993) and considerable discrepancy exists between the career aspirations of young women and their career expectations (Geller, 1996; Sayer & Ellis, 1986). As a result, the skills needed to promote successful transitions to adulthood are likely quite different for adolescent males and females. Handicapped youth and youth from non-majority cultural backgrounds face particular barriers that require differing skill sets in order to facilitate success. Such observations illustrate that is no one pathway that is best for youth: young people in differing contexts have very different transition experiences that require very different transition skills.

Transition needs to be viewed from a life-course perspective. There is much individual variation in the speed and pace of transition processes. Therefore, intervention needs to take into account different contextual factors and different people factors. Different kinds of interventions are needed for different kinds of people in different kinds of contexts. Moreover, intervention needs to be developmental, proactive and preventive, not just remedial. Intervention needs to look at people's capacities and to let people know when they are doing OK. Furthermore, because adolescent-to-adult transitions really begin "pre-youth," interventions also need to begin early in order to be successful. Multidisciplinary, multisectoral and multidimensional approaches need to be developed in order to embrace the broad range of personal and contextual factors involved in promoting successful transitions.

The reality is that most youth are doing OK, many youth could use some help, some youth need very little help, a small number of youth need intensive help. We need a cross section of methodological approaches, utilizing multiple measures, developed and conducted collaboratively in order to discover how to facilitate success, keeping in mind that there are multiple levels of success and success may look quite different to different people. We need to strengthen and reinforce individual and community resources, while minimizing the threats, barriers and impeding forces. This can only be done if we recognize the new societal context and develop comprehensive approaches that meet individual and group needs. The payoffs of helping youth make successful transitions to fulfilling and productive lives is worth the investment.

References

Advisory Group on Working Time and the Distribution of Work. (1994). *Report of the Advisory Group on Working Time and the Distribution of Work.* Ottawa, ON: Minister of Supply and Services Canada.

Allen, S. & Hiebert, B. (1991). "Stress and coping in adolescents." *Canadian Journal of Counseling,* 25, 19-32.

Arthur, N. (1997). "Counselling issues with international students." *Canadian Journal of Counselling,* 31, 259-274.

Arthur, N. & Hiebert, B. (1996). "Coping with the transition to post-secondary education." *Canadian Journal of Counselling,* 30, 93-103.

Badets, J. (1993). "Canada's immigrants: Recent trends." *Canadian Social Trends,* 29, 8-11.

Bezanson, M. L. & Hopkins, K. S. (1998). *Building better career futures.* Ottawa, ON: Canadian Career Development Foundation.

Chadsey-Rusch, J., Rusch, F. R. & O'Reilly, M. F. (1991). "Transition from school to integrated communities." *RASE: Remedial And Special Education,* 12(6), 23-33.

Clark, W. (1997, Spring). "School leavers revisited." *Canadian Social Trends,* 44, 10-12.

Collins, S. &, Angen, M. (1997). "Adolescents voice their needs: Implications for health promotion on suicide prevention." *Canadian Journal of Counseling,* 31, 53-66.

Collins, S. & Hiebert, B. (1995). "Coping with the future: Challenging traditional beliefs about what adolescents need." In M. Van Norman (Ed.). *Natcon 21* (pp. 91-99). Toronto, ON: University of Toronto Career Centre.

Compas, B. E., Malcarne, V. L. & Fondacaro, K. M. (1988). "Coping with stressful events in older children and young adolescents." *Journal of Consulting and Clinical Psychology,* 56, 405-411.

D'Arcy, C. (1982). "Prevalence and correlates of nonpsychotic psychiatric symptoms in the general population." *Canadian Journal of Psychiatry,* 27, 316-324.

D'Arcy, C. & Siddique, C. M. (1984). "Psychological distress among Canadian adolescents." *Psychological Medicine,* 14, 615-628.

Day, B., Redekopp, D. & Robb, M. (1994). *Engage.* Edmonton, AB: Centre for Career Development Innovation, Concordia University College.

Foot, D. (1996). *Boom, bust, and echo: How to profit from the coming demographic shift.* Toronto, ON: Macfarlane, Walter & Ross.

Frank, J. (1996). *After high school: The first years – The first report of the school leavers follow-up survey, 1995.* Ottawa, ON: Minister of Public Works and Government Services.

Gabor, P., Thibodeau, S. & Manychief, S. (1996). "Taking flight: The experiences and perceptions of native youth in independent living." In B. Galaway & J. Hudson (Eds.), *Youth in transition to adulthood: Research and policy implication* (pp. 79-89). Toronto, ON: Thompson Educational Publishing.

Geller, G. (1996). "Educational, occupational, and family aspirations of women: A longitudinal study." In B. Galaway & J. Hudson (Eds.), *Youth in transition to adulthood: Research and policy implication* (pp. 107-117). Toronto, ON: Thompson Educational Publishing.

Good, T. L. & Brophy, J. E. (1978). *Looking in classrooms*. New York: Springer.
Hackett, H. & Baran, D. (1995). "Canadian action on early school leaving: The national Stay-in-School initiative." In B. Hiebert (Ed.). *Exemplary career development programs and practices: The best from Canada*. Greensboro, NC: ERIC/CASS.
Hiebert, B. (1983). "A framework for planning stress control interventions." *Canadian Counsellor*, 17, 51-61.
Hiebert, B. (1988). "Controlling stress: A conceptual update." *Canadian Journal of Counselling*, 22, 226-241.
Hiebert, B. (1991). "Nature and treatment of stress-related problems in schools." In R. Short, L. Stewin & S. McCann (Eds.). *Educational psychology in Canada* (pp. 210-232). Toronto ON: MacMillan.
Hiebert, B. (1998). *Creating a working alliance*. Athabasca, AB: Athabasca University.
Hiebert, B. & Huston, M. (1992, Spring). "Adolescent perceptions: What stresses kids and how they cope." *Applying Research to the Classroom*, 10(2), 2-7.
Hiebert, B., Collins, S. & Cairns, K. V. (1994). "What do adolescents need: Adult versus student perceptions." In M. Van Norman (Ed.) *Natcon-20: National Consultation on Vocational Counselling Papers*. (199-207). Toronto, ON: University of Toronto Career Centre.
Hiebert, B., Jarvis, P., Bezanson, L., Ward, V. & Hearn, J. (1992). "CAMCRY: Meeting the needs of Canadian Youth." In M. Van Norman (Ed.) *Natcon-18: National Consultation on Vocational Counselling Papers*. (pp. 33-39). Toronto, ON: University of Toronto Career Centre.
Hiebert, B., Kemeny, K. & Kurchak, W. (in press). "Guidance-related needs of junior high school students." *Guidance and Counselling*.
Holmes, J. & Silverman, E. L. (1992). *We're here, listen to us! A survey of young women in Canada*. Ottawa, ON: Canadian Advisory Council on the Status of Women.
Hoyt, K. B. (1988). "The changing work force: A review of projections – 1986 to 2000." *The Career Development Quarterly*, 37, 31-39.
Hoyt, K. B. (1991). "The concept of work: Bedrock for career development." *Future Choices*, 23-29.
Lazarus, R. S. & Folkman, S. (1984). *Stress, appraisal, and coping*. New York: Springer.
Lehr, R. & Jeffery, G. (1996). "Career support needs of youth: A qualitative analysis of the rural perspective." *Canadian Journal of Counselling*, 30, 240-253.
Lessard, J. J. (in press). "Adolescent stress and workload: From bamboo seed to flying." *Guidance and Counselling*.
Mailandt, W. (in press). "Adolescent perception of workload and stress." *Guidance and Counselling*.
Martin, F. E. (1996). "Tales of transition: Gender differences in managing eighteen." In B. Galaway & J. Hudson (Eds.), *Youth in transition to adulthood: Research and policy implication* (pp. 99-106). Toronto, ON: Thompson Educational Publishing.
Martin, J. & Martin, W. (1983). *Personal development: Self-instruction for personal agency*. Calgary, AB: Detselig.

Mitchell, B. A. & Gee, E. M. (1996). "Young adults returning home: Implications for social policy." In B. Galaway & J. Hudson (Eds.), *Youth in transition to adulthood: Research and policy implication* (pp. 61-71). Toronto, ON: Thompson Educational Publishing.

Muuss, R. E. (1988). *Theories of adolescence.* New York, NY: McGraw-Hill.

Neimeyer, G. (Ed.). (1993). *Constructivist assessment: A casebook.* Newbury Park, CA: Sage.

NWT Department of Education, Culture & Employment. (1997). *NWT labour force development plan: A workable approach.* Yellowknife, NWT: Government of the Northwest Territories.

O'Reilly, E. & Alfred, D. (1995). *Making career sense of labour market information.* Ottawa, ON: Canadian Career Development Foundation.

Peavy, R. V. (1992). "A constructivist model of training for career counselors." *Journal of Career Development,* 19, 215-228

Peavy, R. V. (1996). "Constructivist career counselling and assessment." *Guidance & Counselling,* 11(3), 8-14.

Perron, J. (1996). "Ethnicity and educational aspirations of high-school students." In B. Galaway & J. Hudson (Eds.), *Youth in transition to adulthood: Research and policy implication* (pp. 127-135). Toronto, ON: Thompson Educational Publishing.

Petersen, A. C. & Spiga, R. (1982). "Adolescence and stress." In L. Goldberg & S. Breznitz (Eds.), *Handbook of stress: Theoretical and clinical aspects* (pp. 515-528). New York: The Free Press.

Posterski, D. & Bibby, R. (1988). *Canada's youths: "Ready for today": A comprehensive survey of 15-24 year olds.* Ottawa, ON: The Canadian Youth Foundation.

Price, J. H. (1985). "A model for explaining adolescent stress." *Health Education,* 16, 36-40.

Redekopp, D. E., Day, B. & Robb, M. (1995). "The 'High Five' of career development." In B. Hiebert (Ed.). *Exemplary career development programs and practices: The best from Canada.* Greensboro, NC: ERIC/CASS.

Roberts, K. & Parsell, G. (1992). "Entering the labour market in Britain: The survival of traditional opportunity structures." *Sociological Review,* 40, 726-753.

Savickas, M. L. & Lent, R. W. (1997). *Convergence in career development theories: Implications for science and practice.* Palo Alto, CA: Consulting Psychologist Press.

Sayer, L. A. (1993). *The acappella papers: Careers and future plans of young women in Canada.* Ottawa, ON: Canadian Teachers' Federation.

Sayer, L. & Ellis, D. (1986). *When I grow up... Career expectations and aspirations of Canadian school children.* Ottawa, ON: Women's Bureau, Labour Canada.

Schaie, W. K. & Willis, S. L. (1986). *Adult development and aging.* Boston, MS: Little Brown.

Super, D. E. (1987). "Career and life development." In D. Brown & L. Brooks (Eds.). *Career choice and development.* San Francisco, CA: Jossey-Bass.

Thoresen, C. E. & Eagleston, J. R. (1983). "Chronic stress in children and adolescents." *Theory into Practice,* 22, 48-56.

Travis, L. D. & Violato, C. (1989). "Experience, mass media use and beliefs about youth: A comparative study." In C. Violato & A. Marini (Eds.),

Child development: Readings for teachers (pp. 375-390). Calgary, Alberta: Detselig Enterprises.

Unrau, Y. & Krysik, J. (1996). "Research on preparation for intimacy and family life: Research and policy implications." In B. Galaway & J. Hudson (Eds.), *Youth in transition to adulthood: Research and policy implication* (pp. 238-243). Toronto, ON: Thompson Educational Publishing.

Violato, C. & Holden, W. B. (1988) "A confirmatory factor analysis of a four factor model of adolescent concerns." *Journal of Youth and Adolescence*, 17, 101-113.

Chapter 2
Managing Cross-Cultural Transitions

Nancy Arthur

Cultural Diversity is a Current Reality

Demographic changes are reflected by the cultural diversity of Canada's population. National policies of multiculturalism have encouraged citizens to maintain their unique cultural backgrounds while sharing Canadian citizenship (Berry, 1994; Esses & Gardner, 1996). Apart from demographic changes, Canadians are also facing major challenges in responding to the marketplace of a global economy. This includes business transactions with people from diverse cultural backgrounds in both Canadian and foreign settings. As borders of trade, travel and immigration shift throughout the world, there is increased interest in the experiences of people who work, study and live in cross-cultural settings (Goodman, 1994; Ward & Kennedy, 1993). Responding to the current realities of cultural diversity requires people to have an understanding of cultural transitions and strategies for cross-cultural effectiveness. Concurrently, employers, counsellors and other professionals must be familiar with ways to prepare people for managing cross-cultural transitions.

This chapter describes the nature of transitions with a focus on the people whose living, working and learning circumstances require adjustment to cross-cultural contexts. The nature of cross-cultural transitions are impacted by dimensions of voluntariness, mobility and permanence (Berry, 1997). Some people embark upon cross-cultural transitions voluntarily or involuntarily due to extenuating personal or political circumstances. Transitions may require permanent residence or exposure to changing cultural contexts on a temporary basis. The groups highlighted in this chapter include First Nations people, immigrants and refugees, workers in Canadian and foreign settings, and international students. Two qualifiers are in order. First, the selection of these particular groups should not preclude studies of other Canadians who are in cultural transition (e.g., specific ethnic minority groups, gays and lesbians, persons with disabilities). Second, this is a chapter written from a generalist perspective in which common experiences are detailed. The actual experiences of individuals are likely to contain considerable intragroup variation. Nonetheless, the chapter is intended to be a starting point for exploring the nature of transitions and the experiences of individuals and families whose lives are impacted by shifting cultural forces. The chapter ends with a discussion of key issues for preparing people to manage cross-cultural transitions.

Transition as a Process of Cultural Change

Transitions involve a process in which individuals experience a change in their personal assumptions or world view (Schlossberg, 1984, 1992). During cross-cultural transition, exposure to norms and behavior that contrast with one's own culture poses challenges to an individual's understanding of self, values or assumptions about others (Ishiyama, 1995; Zaharna, 1989). The adjustment to new cultural contexts can result in profound learning.

The transition between original and new cultural contexts has been depicted as a process of culture shock (Oberg, 1960; Winkelman, 1994). Early studies described culture shock using a U-curve model of adjustment (Lysgaard, 1955) with three stages: Contact with the host culture, conflict with the host culture and adaptation. Stages progress from initial excitement and optimism about the new culture, a shift toward the bottom of the U-curve to reflect cross-cultural difficulties and resulting negative effects, and the later stage of recovery as strategies for managing in the host culture are mastered. A revised W-curve model of culture shock (Gullahorn & Gullahorn, 1963) has a stage to account for the adjustment of returning to the original culture. Culture shock may manifest in psychological symptoms such as depression, social withdrawal, concentration and performance inhibition, loneliness and reactions such as hostility. Culture shock may also include physiological reactions such as insomnia, gastrointestinal problems and other physical conditions (Thomas & Althen, 1989; Winkelman, 1994).

The stages of culture shock are helpful in considering how people adjust over time. People in cross-cultural transition are immediately immersed into situations that require learning and adjustment to new role demands. Disruptions to familiar ways of interacting and usual sources of personal validation, along with the need for rapid acquisition of culturally-appropriate responses, lead to the sense of confusion and conflict associated with culture shock (Ishiyama, 1995; Pedersen, 1991; Winkelman, 1994).

Although models of culture shock have alerted us to the shifting nature of cross-cultural transitions, they are limited by the lack of attention paid to individual differences. For example, the models do not incorporate the varying levels of adjustment with which people enter new cultural contexts and the prominence of different experiences over time. People's coping responses must also be examined in order to account for either positive or negative adaptation (Lazarus, 1997; Searle & Ward, 1990). The focus on intrapersonal variables (e.g., previous cross-cultural experience, personal flexibility) may obscure interpersonal dynamics (e.g., interactions with foreigners, attitudes about particular cultural groups) that impact adjustment. In order to understand the nature of cross-cultural transitions, both factors within the person and factors within the cultural environment must be taken into account (Furham & Bochner, 1986; Lazarus, 1997).

Acculturation and Adaptation in Cross-Cultural Transitions

A framework that has been applied extensively to cross-cultural transitions is the process of acculturation (Berry, 1997; Berry, Mindle, Mok, 1987). The concept of acculturation refers to psychological change during cross-cultural transition that results in adaptation to the new cultural context (Berry, 1997). This perspective supports the position that acculturative stress results when demands of the new cultural context exceed personal coping resources (Berry, 1997; Lazarus, 1997). Depending upon factors such as the scope and severity of new cultural demands and the individual's capacity for learning new cultural competencies, acculturative stress may be experienced as minor adjustment problems or range to serious psychological disturbances (Berry & Kim, 1988). Cross-cultural transitions are complex with interrelated factors involving psychological, socio-cultural and economic adaptations. Psychological adaptation refers to a set of internal psychological outcomes such as a clear sense of personal identity, positive mental health and personal satisfaction in the new cultural context (Berry, 1997; Searle & Ward, 1990). In contrast to psychological outcomes, socio-cultural adaptation refers to external psychological outcomes resulting from an individual's skills for managing social areas such as family, work or learning roles (Berry, 1997; Ward & Kennedy, 1993). Employment is also critical for personal satisfaction and economic viability in a new culture (Berry, 1997).

Research on acculturation stress indicates substantial variation between individuals and groups in their degree of cross-cultural adaptation (Berry et al., 1987; Ward & Kennedy, 1993). Four acculturation strategies are based upon the extent to which cultural identity is maintained and the extent to which individuals engage in participation with other cultural groups (Berry, 1997). First, individuals who either do not want to or who are unable to hold on to their original cultural identity adopt a position of assimilation to new cultural ways. Second, individuals who hold on to their original cultural identity and do not participate in new cultural contexts adopt a position of separation. Third, the lack of available avenues for maintaining traditional cultural identity and barriers to joining new cultural systems results in a sense of exclusion or marginalization. The fourth acculturation strategy of integration refers to an interest in maintaining some degree of one's original culture while participating as an active member of the new cultural context. A key assumption that must be challenged is the expectation of the dominant culture for non-dominant groups to assimilate to their cultural point of view. Power differences between the dominant group and smaller cultural groups may create pressure for assimilation as a condition of group participation. Integration, in the true spirit of bi-cultural interaction, requires motivation on the part of both groups to negotiate common understandings and to engage in new forms of behavior.

The Re-entry Transition

The process of readjusting to one's home culture has received less attention than the initial entry stage of cross-cultural transition. Reacculturation has been addressed from four areas of adjustment: Challenge to self-concept, values conflict, unfulfilled expectations and a sense of loss (Austin, 1986; Wang, 1997).

Socialization to a new cultural context involves gradual exposure to new perspectives. As people in cross-cultural transition experience different values, they are challenged to examine their personal cultural beliefs. People may feel conflicted about old ways of understanding the world and new insights. Struggling for belonging between two cultural contexts can be experienced as marginalization (Wang, 1997). Many people also experience a sense of loss in the transition from one culture to another. After exposure to a new culture, people acquire a sense of attachment to relationships, daily routines in work or study roles, and to other lifestyle factors (Wang, 1997). Anticipation about returning home may coincide with a sense of loss about leaving aspects of culture behind.

For many individuals, returning home is a disappointing transition. This can be explained by unrealistic expectations and lack of awareness by both individuals and their significant others regarding adjustments required by re-entry transition. Discrepancies between expectations and the realities of returning home can prompt further reflections about cultural beliefs and practices. The cumulative changes that have occurred in self and others during the period of contact with another culture can have long-standing implications for personal adaptation. Depending upon the degree of personal change and change in the home culture, dissonance may lead people to wonder if they can ever feel at home again. Consequently, readjusting to one's home culture may be the most difficult period of cross-cultural transition (Adler, 1975; Martin, 1984, 1986; Wang, 1997).

Families in Cross-Cultural Transition

The majority of literature on cross-cultural transition has focused on individual adjustment and adaptation while neglecting the impact of new cultural contexts on families (Mallinckrodt & Leong, 1992). Issues such as status and role changes, language proficiency, legal ability to work, social isolation and even loss of contact with individual members may be paramount for family adaptation. What is unique about the circumstances of many families in cross-cultural transition is the need to reconcile living bi-culturally while maintaining traditional family values and practices (Baptiste, 1990). Differential rates of acculturation between family members can lead to conflict. Children typically have more opportunities for interaction in the dominant culture, therefore, their acculturation occurs at a faster rate than that of older family members. As a consequence of uprooting and responding to new cultural demands, role reversals and shifting boundaries can lead to changing expectations between family members. Due to exposure to new norms for behavior, traditional gender role expectations may be challenged. When the roles of parents are reversed, or children need to take on responsibilities traditionally allocated to adults, conflict may escalate. Families already taxed by other transition demands may also experience distress about shifting family roles (Baptiste, 1993).

The potential for marital and intergenerational conflict exists when some members of the family wish to maintain original family values while other family members want to adopt the values and lifestyles of a new cultural context. Parents may interpret new behavior as a sign that children are moving away from core family values. Increasing interest in the opinions of teachers, new friends or co-workers may escalate the level of family conflict. In an effort to maintain the values and traditions of the family unit, activities and contact with members of the new culture may be restricted (Baptiste, 1993).

Many of the issues voiced by families in cross-cultural transition suggest a paradox embedded in the acculturation process (Baptiste, 1993). On the one hand, the majority of people enter new cultural contexts in order to improve their circumstances. Goals for a "better future" must be accompanied by achievement in areas such as education and employment. A paradox exists, because in order for people to be successful, a corresponding degree of cultural integration is necessary (e.g., making new friends, acquiring language proficiency, practicing values of the dominant culture) (Baptiste, 1990). Discrepant views by family members is more than conflict per se, it represents the struggle in problem-solving between the family's original culture and options available in new cultural contexts (Arthur, 1998a).

Cross-Cultural Transition: Opportunities for Learning

Cross-cultural transitions often pose difficult issues for individual and family adjustment. Despite all of the negative implications, the transition experience provides individuals with vast opportunities for learning new ways of relating and responding in cross-cultural contexts (Anderson, 1994; Berry, 1997). It is through cross-cultural transitions that people transform views about their own culture and the world around them. While this process may require letting go of certain cultural ways and behavior, i.e., cultural shedding (Berry, 1992), to fit in with new expectations, cross-cultural transitions also entail cultural learning. Through personal observations and interactions with others with culturally diverse backgrounds, people have the potential to learn in multicultured ways that can lead to positive development. The shifting forces of cultural transition impact people's lives in complex ways. The discussion will now turn to groups of people for whom cross-cultural transition has been a major influence on their development.

First Nations People in Transition

Considered as a separate designated group under the Employment Equity Act of Canada, Aboriginal people include North American Indians, Inuit and Metis. Estimates of population based upon birth rates and reinstatements based on Bill C-31 amendments to the Indian Act indicate that people of Aboriginal ancestry currently comprise more than 4% of the Canadian population. Aboriginal population growth rates by regional distribution in the Prairie provinces, Yukon and Northwest Territories are expected to reach 16%, 24% and 67%, respectively, by the year 2016 (Esses & Gardner, 1996; Statistics Canada, 1995). For the purpose of this discussion, the titles Aboriginal and Native will be used interchangeably to refer to the First Nations people of Canada.

Canada's Aboriginal people have endured a history of transition and adjustment throughout the settlement of this country. Comparisons to other groups in cross-cultural transition (e.g., immigrants, refugees, international students) demonstrate that Aboriginal people experience relatively high levels of acculturative stress (Berry, et al., 1987). In order to appreciate the issues faced by Aboriginal people in cultural transition, their history of oppression must be acknowledged. Conflicts between the values and practices of traditional Aboriginal culture and the demands of dominant Canadian society have resulted in serious social problems in areas of health, education, employment and economic status. Increasing attention is paid to events suffered by Aboriginal people through colonization and ways to overcome long-standing issues of cultural oppression.

In order to understand the transition issues of Aboriginal people, it is essential to appreciate the cultural bases of behavior between Native and Non-Natives in North America (Herring, 1996). The emphasis on interconnectedness in traditional Native culture can be seen in the values of sharing, harmony with nature, present time orientation, cooperation with the group and extended family, holistic approach to health, present time orientation, noninterference and respect for elders (Herring, 1996; McCormick, 1997). In contrast, the dominant Eurocentric cultural values in North America emphasize individualism, competition and domination, future time orientation, individualism, mastery over nature, focus on youth and preference for scientifically-based explanations. Although factors such as tribal affiliation, the changing and diverse roles of women, and levels of acculturation impact cultural adherence (LaFromboise, Heyle & Ozer, 1990; Restoule, 1997), there have been many pressures for Natives to assimilate to the dominant culture.

The history of Canada's First Nations people is filled with efforts to dominate and eliminate their traditional cultural values and practices. Perhaps the most pervasive example is the residential school experience. Children were separated from their families, forced to abandon their language and cultural rituals, and comply with the ways of the dominant society. Efforts to forcibly assimilate children have led to accusations of "cultural genocide" (Bull, 1991). What happened in residential schools? As relayed to the author by one former resident, "They taught us to hate ourselves." The traumatic experiences of First Nations children in residential schools have left a legacy of intergenerational effects for the health of both individuals and their families (Morrisette, 1994). The rejection of Native values has compounded a sense of personal and social isolation, as well as despair about the future. Low self esteem and above average rates of substance abuse and suicide among First Nations people have been attributed to the consequences of cultural oppression (Green, 1997).

The internalized shame about their cultural identity has left many First Nations people in a state of transition. Youth face the dilemma of feeling caught between two worlds, maintaining loyalty to Native culture while desiring to be a part of the dominant culture (Morrisette, 1994). This issue is pronounced for youth who seek access to economic success through educational and employment opportunities. The limited availability of vocational opportunities on reservations has major implications for career development (Leung, 1995). While living on reservations, youth are exposed to a limited scope of vocational opportunities. This results in a lack of knowledge about the world of work and a restricted view of occupational possibilities. As most occupations with higher social status are only available in urban settings, youth are often forced to leave the reservation to gain access to professional opportunities. Access to post-secondary training and education programs almost entirely depends upon moving from the reservation to attend schools in urban settings. Leaving the reservation requires reconciling Native values, dealing with disruptions to the usual support system, and attempting to acculturate to an urban lifestyle. In addition, youth who are socialized on reservations may lack academic and work skills to be successful in the dominant culture (Leung, 1995).

Recent events have focused attention on First Nations people. Confrontation between the Mohawks and the Canadian Army in Quebec, the alleged financial mismanagement of the Stoney Reserve in Alberta and the media attention given to land claims have highlighted current cultural conflicts. The Canadian government is attempting to address the long-standing concerns of First Nations people through the Royal Commission Report on Aboriginal People 1996 (RCAP) (Indian and Northern Affairs, 1996). A statement of reconciliation and apology has been issued for the travesties inflicted through residential schools, along with the announcement of a $350 million fund to support the development of community-based healing. However, the recommendations of RCAP and a subsequent document, *Gathering Strength: Canada's Aboriginal Action Plan* (Indian and Northern Affairs Canada, 1998) are being received with caution. Perhaps the greatest barriers to the success of the recommendations contained in the Report are the long-standing issues of mistrust in relations between Native and non-Native people of Canada (France, 1997). Recent attention has also been paid to the health promotion of First Nations people, including areas of spiritual, physical and psychological health (France, 1997; Ross & Ross, 1992). Through locating and recognizing strengths in Native culture, efforts are being made to reconnect Natives to their cultural heritage and to help them gain greater control in their lives. It appears as if the future of First Nations people is contingent upon their abilities to restore the strengths of their cultural heritage while negotiating opportunities in collaboration with members of the larger Canadian society. Aboriginal groups deserve to be recognized for their contribution to multiculturalism in Canada. There are tremendous benefits to be derived from recognizing the strengths of Native culture and from resolving differences that have historically divided the people of Canada.

Immigrants and Refugees

Changes in immigration policy account for increasing diversity in the ethnic composition of Canada. While the immigration rate has remained relatively stable throughout the last two decades, the proportion of immigrants coming from source countries has changed (Esses & Gardner, 1996). In the earlier part of the century, the majority of immigrants arrived from Europe and North America; however, over the last three decades, source countries have extended to Asia and the Middle East, the Caribbean, Americas and Africa (Statistics Canada, 1995). These varied groups have introduced diverse cultural backgrounds and customs to Canadian society.

The adaptation of immigrants is impacted by factors ranging from the individual's resources to national policies (Berry, 1997). The experiences of immigrants are highly variable due to circumstances surrounding the reasons for immigration, language proficiency, education, and access to financial and support resources (Berry et al., 1987; Westwood & Ishiyama, 1991). As a general rule, the greater the difference in the cultural norms of the source country and new Canadian lifestyles, the greater the degree of adjustment required in the transition of immigration (Berry, 1997). Uprooting and relocating to another country is a disorienting experience. Adjustment involves not only coping with new customs and unfamiliar expectations, but also the loss of familiar people and ways of living. Some immigrants lack essential language comprehension and communication skills for basic roles and services. It has also been documented that immigrants face employment barriers due to language competency, problems in transferring credentials between countries, lack of familiarity with employment systems, and systemic racism in social and employment practices (Westwood & Ishiyama, 1991). Optimism about life in Canada may be tempered by educational and employment barriers.

Acceptance and support for new immigrants also depends upon the felt sense of security in the lives of Canadians. Fluctuations in the economy lead to intense competition for employment and other economic resources. Stereotypes and racist attitudes can be linked to economic fears and the belief that immigrants "take jobs" from other Canadians (Palmer, 1996). Without education about the current role of immigration in our society, discrimination will continue to be barrier for new Canadians.

The cross-cultural transition of immigration begins with the decision to leave the home country and seek residence in Canada. Post-migration adjustment has been linked to the extent to which relocation is a voluntary decision (Berry, 1997). A hallmark distinction of refugees is that immigration to another country is not a preferred choice; it is involuntary migration because of fear of persecution (Bemak, Chung & Bornemann, 1996). Many refugees are exposed to life-threatening or traumatic events during the transition process (Arredondo, Orjuela & Moore, 1989). In the premigration stage, there may be conditions of violence and trauma experienced by individuals, families or entire communities. During the actual migration era, there is heightened fear related to the means of escaping and the possibility of being apprehended. Refugees exposed to trauma, either directly or vicariously, often manifest severe stress reactions that lead to recurring crises of adjustment (Arthur & Ramaliu, in press). During the post-migration stage, refugees must simultaneously deal with the upheaval of adjustment to a new culture and their experience of pre-migration trauma. Unresolved trauma issues can immobilize refugees from dealing with the tasks of managing in a new culture (Strober, 1994).

Despite the level of choice to leave their native country, family members are likely to have varying sentiments about living in Canada. When individual family members would have preferred to stay in their country of origin, there is likely to be a higher level of conflict in the family. If individual family members experience losses in status in important life arenas (e.g., peers, employment level, racism), negative sentiments can lead to disputes between family members regarding their current lifestyle (Baptiste, 1990).

The immigration process for adults is generally more difficult than for young children, primarily due to the differential rate of language acquisition and the insulating support of family (Berry, 1997). However, the needs of youth in cultural transition should not be ignored. Youth must also adjust to demands such as loss of former peers and making new friends, differences in educational systems and teaching methodologies, role adjustments in the family and learning culturally appropriate ways of behaving (Kopala, Esquivel & Baptiste, 1994). Given these commonly reported transition demands, it must also be acknowledged that not every immigrant will experience cross-cultural transitions similarly, with the same intensity, nor will this process necessarily lead to major problems of adjustment. Despite adverse conditions associated with their cross-cultural transition, most immigrants positively adapt to life in Canada.

As a nation of immigrants, Canadians have taken pride in their tolerance of diversity (Esses & Gardner, 1986). However, as immigration policies broaden the scope of ethnic origins, programs must be in place to support cultural integration. Immigrants and refugees require a multidimensional response in which resources are mobilized at the levels of resettlement services, education and employment services, professional resources and local community host programs (Arthur & Ramaliu, in press). However, without corresponding efforts to educate Canadians about immigration practices and ways to bridge cultural differences, levels of tolerance will become taxed. Responsive community programs have much to contribute towards promoting positive relations between Canadians of diverse ethnic backgrounds.

Workers in Local and Foreign Settings

Canada's labor force reflects the cultural diversity of its citizens. Employers are challenged to respond to the needs of employees whose capacity for effective work relationships is essential for organizational success (Granrose & Oskamp, 1997). Organizations need to ensure that employees from culturally diverse backgrounds are aware of cultural influences on their behavior. Otherwise, people display ethnocentrism when they do not incorporate culturally relevant information about themselves and others (Daniels & D'Andrea, 1996). Without an understanding of the cultural influences surrounding work place behavior, perceived differences tend to exacerbate conflict (Singelis & Pedersen, 1997). Knowledge about other cultural groups can assist workers to develop informed perspectives about both similarities and differences between people.

In addition to cultural diversity within organizations, broader changes in the world of work are challenging Canadians to be culturally responsive. Increased access to national economies has motivated many organizations to internationalize. There are expanding international employment opportunities for Canadians in both domestic and foreign settings. The expansion of organizations into the global marketplace has focused attention on worker adjustment to foreign cultures. Workers on foreign assignments are often chosen for their technical expertise; however, their capacity for positive cross-cultural adaptation is equally important. Inadequate adaptation to the international work place is costly to both organizations and individuals (Parker & McEvoy, 1993). A prolonged negative cross-cultural experience and/or prematurely returning home may lead to serious consequences (Harrison, Chadwick & Scales, 1996). Preparing workers for the realities of international work requires an understanding about the nature of cross-cultural transitions and strategies for cross-cultural effectiveness.

Predeparture programs typically focus on providing information to workers about aspects of the foreign culture (Saphiere, 1996). Training programs should also be designed to enhance awareness about the ways in which the personal culture of workers impacts their view of foreign environments. Ethnocentric attitudes impede cross-cultural adjustment and the flexibility that is necessary for cross-cultural effectiveness (Searle & Ward, 1990). One criticism of pre-departure programs is that providing too much cultural information can lead to a false sense of competency. However, when people are expected to work in foreign cultures with large discrepancies from their home culture, it is unlikely that programs can go too far in their level of preparation (Parker & Envoy, 1993; Rogers & Ward, 1993). Programs cannot prevent people from experiencing acculturative stress. It is vital that workers have a framework for understanding and responding to their experience of cross-cultural transition (Brislin & Yoshida, 1994; Ward & Kennedy, 1993).

Organizations must also prepare workers for effective relations on international work teams. The need for effective cross-cultural interactions has led to an expanded focus of orientation programs from preparation for working in foreign environments to "inpatriation" programs designed to prepare foreign workers for managing in the local environment (Harvey, 1997). Without training programming to bridge cultural differences, interpersonal problems can jeopardize the success of international projects (Kealey & Prothoe, 1996; Saphiere, 1996).

Relationships with both co-nationals and foreigners are also important for personal adjustment during cross-cultural transitions. Social support acts as a buffer against the psychological effects of stress experienced by people in crossing cultures (Searle & Ward, 1990). Access to support for problem-solving can assist workers to broaden their perspective about available coping strategies. As the demands of international assignments involve working in unfamiliar situations, where usual sources of social support are not available, workers may need assistance to identify alternate coping strategies.

Organizations are faced with many challenges in preparing workers for the realities of cultural diversity both within local and international settings. As the nature of work changes, employees must be prepared to adjust to different job responsibilities and performance expectations. Changes in the work environment require employees to respond to shifting demands in local settings as well as the new challenges associated with living and working in foreign environments. Cutting across these organizational and environmental factors is the need for employees to have effective skills for interacting with people whose background and experience are different from their own. The changing world of work requires that employees possess a repertoire of cultural competencies for managing their career development (Herr, 1993). As Canada's population and economy becomes increasingly interdependent upon people from other nations, the future of work is strongly influenced by the capacity of workers to manage cross-cultural transitions.

International Students

Educators across Canada are faced with the challenge of preparing students for future roles in changing cultural contexts (Herr, 1993; Zussman & Poapst, 1995). International education represents a relatively untapped source of expertise in educating Canadians regarding diverse cultural and professional practices in other countries (Arthur, 1997). Along with global education initiatives, increasing efforts are directed at the recruitment of international students to Canadian schools and to opportunities for Canadians to study in other countries (Knight, 1994). Understanding the nature of cross-cultural transitions for international students is essential for designing effective academic and support programs.

International students "begin" the transition process through applying to foreign institutions, acquiring immigration authorization, gathering financial and other resources, making travel arrangements, and preparing to leave family and friends. Prior to arriving in the host country, international students invest considerable effort into their cross-cultural experience. Their status as temporary sojourners in a foreign country for the duration of an academic program is a unique condition of their cross-cultural experience.

There is tremendous variability in the academic and personal preparation of international students (Arthur, 1997). Expectations for academic performance may not be in line with former achievement levels or foreign teaching methodologies. While international students, like domestic students, are adjusting to role demands in the transition to post-secondary education, this adjustment is further complicated by cultural differences. Given the sheer number of countries and cultures involved in international education, students will not experience cross-cultural transitions equally stressfully. In cases of major differences in the educational and social customs between students' country of origin and the host country, the new cultural context can precipitate major adjustments (Pedersen, 1991).

The common adjustment concerns of international students include educational concerns, language difficulties, financial problems, social isolation, interpersonal difficulties, homesickness, worries about extended family and differences in social customs (Church, 1982; Crano & Crano, 1993; Parr, Bradley & Bingi, 1992; Wehrly, 1988). Language proficiency has been linked to both the academic and social adjustment of international students (Hayes & Lin, 1994; Pedersen, 1991). Students' abilities for language communication and comprehension impact academic progress, students' confidence about approaching academic staff and peers, and the quality of interactions with other people in the host culture (Arthur, 1997). Beyond the issues of internal psychological adjustment, international students are also exposed to external factors such discrimination and racism (Dei, 1992). Gender role expectations for behavior may be challenged by new ways of interacting, leading to experimentation with new behavior and/or problems with sexual harassment (Tyler & Boxer, 1996). These adjustment issues of international students can act as impediments to the attainment of educational and personal goals. Due to the contingency of immigration status based upon academic success, the threat of failure can be an immense pressure (Arthur, 1997).

International students can also be considered as people in social transition. Homesickness and concerns about the well-being of their friends and family can be especially difficult aspects of cross-cultural transition. Anxieties about language proficiency and socially appropriate behavior are inhibitors for developing local networks of social support. Paradoxically, the pressures of managing new academic demands and studying in a second language may prevent international students from participating in social programming that is intended to support their experience of transition.

While international students may desire more contact with Canadian students, the quality of social interactions may intensify the sense of social alienation (Arthur, 1997). International students may find relationships in Canadian culture to be confusing and lacking the intimacy that leads to a sense of belonging. Barriers such as language competencies and time in the new culture require effort to overcome cultural misunderstandings and discover mutually rewarding ways of interacting. However, difficulties in forming friendships are also attributable to a lack of understanding by Canadian students (Arthur, 1997). Without cross-cultural training, most students lack competencies for effective cross-cultural relationships.

At the end of their academic program, students must manage the transition of going home. For some students, foreign education results in a clearer commitment to values in their home culture. For other international students, learning about alternate cultural values may prompt dissonance about returning home (Arthur, 1997; Uehara, 1986). International students have reported concerns about the transfer of educational and technical expertise, language acquisition, career mobility, local political conditions and "fitting back in" to existing family, educational or employment roles (Brabant,

Palmer & Gramling, 1990; Pedersen, 1990). Adjustment may be compounded by the lack of programming to assist international students with the transition home (Westwood, Lawrence & Paul, 1986).

Perspectives on international student transitions must be connected to larger social and economic changes that are influencing higher education in Canada (Tillett & Lesser, 1992). In a competitive educational marketplace, Canadian institutions are allocating resources to attract greater numbers of international students. In part, there is incentive due to declining funding from government sources and the need to secure alternate funding for educational institutions (Arthur, 1995). However, the value of international education to Canadians is more than an economic resource. International students offer an immense resource of information regarding cultural and academic practices around the world. Ultimately, international education can assist students to prepare for the realities of living, learning and working with people from other cultures.

Competencies for Managing Cross-Cultural Transitions

As detailed throughout this chapter, interaction with people from culturally diverse backgrounds is an integral feature of Canadian society. Many Canadians are faced with daily challenges to manage the cultural differences in school, work place and in surrounding community settings. Other Canadians, for whom educational or employment roles take them to other countries, may find success contingent upon their capacity to adapt to demands in a foreign environment. Shifting social forces require people to have core competencies for managing cross-cultural transitions.

Competencies for training professionals to manage cross-cultural relationships have been outlined in three core areas: Self-awareness, knowledge and skills (Sue, Arredondo & McDavis, 1992). The domain of self-awareness refers to an understanding of the ways in which cultural values influence one's own perceptions and responses during cross-cultural transitions. The domain of knowledge refers to an understanding of the values, beliefs and practices of diverse cultural groups. The skill domain refers to the capacity for culturally responsive behavior. Competencies in all three domains are interrelated for effectively managing cross-cultural transitions.

Self-Awareness Competencies

Personal awareness is a prerequisite for successfully managing cross-cultural transitions. People display ethnocentrism when their behavior is based in culturally specific values and when they do not incorporate culturally relevant information regarding the people around them. In other words, "what people bring" to cross-cultural situations is as critical as factors in the environment. Without acknowledgment of how personal belief systems impact cross-cultural relationships, there is danger of inappropriately judging behavior (Arthur, 1998). A lack of awareness about how one's own values and beliefs impact others can perpetuate issues of racism and alienation in cross-cultural relations, whether this is done intentionally or unintentionally (Pedersen, 1995). Self-awareness is key to understanding the reciprocal influences of culture during interactions with people from diverse backgrounds.

It is noteworthy that members of non-dominant groups are often better informed about the practices and beliefs of dominant cultural groups. As a result of acculturation demands and the need to access resources, non-dominant group members may have more at stake in crossing cultural boundaries. In contrast, members of dominant groups may be less motivated to examine the impact of their values and behavior on others. Rather than taking a stance of blame, it is important to remember that dominance is a role that is learned through the socialization experience (Sue, 1995). As attitudes towards non-dominant groups are also learned through socialization, it bespeaks the need for members of dominant groups to be deliberate about examining the influence of culture in their lives. Without a mutual investment, cross-cultural interactions are likely to be one-sided and perpetuate assimilation rather than integration between cultural groups.

Culture shock is a natural reaction to new cultural contexts. People may approach cross-cultural transitions with a false sense of security due to competencies in other life areas. Novel cross-cultural situations will inevitably require some form of adjustment. General awareness about both psychological and physiological symptoms of culture shock can prevent alarm about unfamiliar reactions and assist to normalize the experience. Understanding one's personal reactions to culture shock, including both psychological and physiological reactions, can be useful for mobilizing appropriate coping strategies.

Regardless of the circumstances that trigger cross-cultural transition, people's view of their situation can either hinder or support their adjustment. It is without question that many transitions include difficult and pervasive life changes. In the middle of a complex change process, it is easy to lose sight of the potential for positive adaptation. However, if people are open-minded to contrasts and alternate points of view, cross-cultural transitions offer tremendous opportunities for personal learning. Although the overwhelming nature of adjustment can consume people's view of their experience, it is important for individuals to consider ways in which the transition is a learning experience. Keeping sight of personal goals and opportunities for growth is a strategy that can offset the difficulties of adjustment and provide motivation for active coping.

The nature of cross-cultural transitions entails a period of dissonance in which personal meanings are challenged. Cross-cultural dissonance may result in a firm grasp on original cultural beliefs and rejection of contrasting values. Where this position is taken and maintained early in the transition experience, the risk is that individuals remain closed to experiencing aspects of the new culture that they may enjoy participating in. A willingness to override personal discomfort and remain open to new experiences can lead to positive outcomes of personal and cultural learning.

Knowledge Competencies

There is growing appreciation of the need for orientation and training programs for people embarking on cross-cultural transitions. Pre-departure and intercultural programs have been developed from the premise that knowledge about other cultures can ease the initial period of adjustment through assisting people to learn about cultural norms for behavior. Without knowledge about the values and beliefs of diverse cultural groups, there is a greater risk of imposing personal biases in ways that are disruptive to cross-cultural relationships (Cushner & Nieman, 1997; Harvey, 1997).

Many cross-cultural training programs use cultural taxonomies (e.g., Hofstede, 1980) to compare and contrast dominant value systems among nations. Through understanding the major dimensions along which culture can be defined, individuals can develop empathy for diverse world views (Brisin & Yoshida, 1994). However, working from the basis of general knowledge about cultural groups also poses the risk of bias through stereotyping. Beyond general cultural assumptions, it is essential that individuals learn how to sensitively inquire about the values and beliefs of others and how to assess the degree to which individuals ascribe to cultural group norms (Grieger & Ponterotto, 1995).

There may be no substitute for the knowledge that can be gained through direct experience with people from culturally diverse backgrounds. With the diversity found in the work places, schools and neighborhoods of our communities, there are many opportunities to gain first-hand knowledge of contrasting cultures. Through deliberate efforts to expand one's usual routine and activities, local communities offer rich resources for gaining knowledge about other cultures.

Skill Competencies

Beyond self-awareness and knowledge about other cultures, people need to be skilled at managing both the interpersonal and intrapersonal dynamics of transition. While many of the coping skills described below are essential for managing in daily living, the demands of working, studying or living in new cultural contexts underscore their importance.

Effective communication skills, including communication between members of the same culture, are critical for success in cross-cultural transitions. As most cross-cultural work or educational projects require effective interactions for success, team-building strategies and strategies for managing interpersonal differences are essential (Saphiere, 1996). Interpersonal relations can become strained with the additional demands of adjusting to new cultural contexts. Effective communication, particularly behavior that enhances group dynamics and problem-solving, is integral for managing transition demands. However, skills that are effective for communicating with people from a similar background may have to be modified for relating to people from culturally diverse backgrounds. Communication for cultural diversity requires competencies for interpreting meanings and responding in culturally appropriate ways (Pedersen & Ivey, 1993; Sue & Sue, 1990).

The exposure to new cultural ways may challenge people's approaches to decision-making. On the one hand, exposure to new values and ways of living may provide individuals with additional opportunities and choices. On the other hand, expanded opportunities may be in conflict with people's traditional ways of approaching life. Any decision that represents a shift in values to the new culture must be carefully reviewed in terms of both the short- and long-term consequences. While an individual may wish to pursue choices available in a new cultural environment, there may be severe and long-lasting consequences for going against the expectations of cultural membership. A central dilemma for decision-making pivots around how far people in cross-cultural transition are prepared to go to preserve traditional values while pursuing goals and opportunities available in the new culture. Ultimately, these decisions could have profound implications for participation in academic, employment or family roles in the future (Arthur, 1998a).

Conflict is an ongoing aspect of interpersonal relationships. Conflict management in cross-cultural relationships is made more complex by two factors. First, the possibility of conflict is greater due to the potential for miscommunication and misunderstandings between people from diverse cultural backgrounds. Secondly, conflict resolution may be more difficult as competing perspectives may pose barriers to identifying mutual interests. Although confrontation and mediation are difficult cross-cultural skills, they are essential for managing cross-cultural transitions.

An innovative approach to conflict and mediation across cultures is the Interpersonal Cultural Grid (Pedersen, 1993; Pedersen & Ivey, 1993; Singelis & Pedersen, 1997). The grid consists of behaviors and expectations in a taxonomy used to demonstrate how people from culturally diverse backgrounds can discover common goals. During cross-cultural interactions, behavior can be misunderstood and become a source of distraction that breaks further communication. However, if the focus can be directed towards the intent of the behavior and shared positive expectations, common ground can be used as the basis from which to negotiate alternatives. Through training people to see beyond differences in behavior and seek the common ground of positive expectancies, they can be assisted to channel conflict into stronger cross-cultural relationships. Effective strategies for negotiating conflict can minimize differences and keep the focus of interactions on similarities and areas of mutual benefit.

Stress management skills have been identified as essential competencies for cross-cultural transitions (Harvey, 1997; Walton, 1990). Skill training in stress management assists with the development of coping strategies to address perceived demands in cross-cultural environments (Walton, 1990). Information regarding cultural expectations and potential adjustment factors may be useful for anticipatory coping (Lazarus & Folkman, 1984). However, it is recommended that cross-cultural training programs also assist individuals to assess their current repertoire for coping with stress. Through self-awareness about the types of situations that one finds stressful and the ways in which coping resources are enacted, an individual can be better prepared to understand their reactions in new cultural contexts, although demands may be different and the usual resources may not be at hand in foreign environments. However, knowledge of the function and forms of coping can assist people to build temporary structures and routines.

As part of a repertoire of stress management skills, social support has been identified as a key coping resource for managing cross-cultural transitions (Searle & Ward, 1990). Social support includes both instrumental (advice, referral to resources) and emotional functions (encouragement, personal validation, expression of effect) (Lazarus & Folkman, 1984). In reaction to cross-cultural situations that appear to be unchangeable, social support can provide a source of personal validation and encouragement (Arthur, 1998c). However, during cross-cultural transition, the more stressed and isolated that individuals feel, the less likely they are to seek assistance with task functions such as work or academic problems. While withdrawal or avoidance may provide short-term relief from locating resources and problem-solving, there may be serious implications for personal, academic or employment outcomes (Arthur, 1997). People's willingness to access social support is also bounded by cultural views of help-seeking. During cross-cultural transitions people may need encouragement to clarify culturally acceptable practices for resolving problems and to identify current impediments for accessing available support systems.

Due to the difficult aspects of acculturation, people tend to lose sight of their progress in managing cross-cultural transitions. Rather than evaluating transition experiences in absolute terms, such as positive and negative or success and failure, evaluations can be applied to specific areas of competency development. Tracking critical incidents, events that are meaningful in people's experience (Brookfield, 1995), offers a useful approach for monitoring cross-cultural transitions (Arthur, 1998c). Consistent with previous work in the field of stress management (Lazarus & Folkman, 1984), critical incidents can be focused on specific demands of cross-cultural adaptation such as interpersonal functioning, morale, somatic illness and the sufficiency of coping strategies. Responses can be used as a stimulus for discussion, provide work teams or family members with feedback, and direct efforts to improve coping in the cross-cultural environment (Arthur, 1998c).

Conclusion

In light of the rapidly changing demographics in our society, it is essential that Canadians become culturally responsive. Change needs to be addressed at both individual and systemic levels. Canadian businesses and educational institutions can no longer afford to operate from perspectives that do not incorporate the needs of culturally diverse workers, students and members of our local communities. The shift from living, learning and working in traditional ways to incorporating cultural differences will require Canadians to examine their values and beliefs and to make considerable changes in ways of interacting with others. The benefits of working together in transition far outweigh the difficulties. It is through cooperation and mutual respect that people can learn about culture from two perspectives, the cultural practices of others and the influences of culture on our own lives.

References

Adler, P. (1975). The transitional experience: An alternative view of culture shock. *Journal of Humanistic Psychology, 15,* 13-23.

Anderson, L. E. (1994). A new look at an old construct: Cross-cultural adaptation. *International Journal of Intercultural Relations, 18,* 293-328.

Arredondo, P., Orjuela, E. & Moore, L. (1989). Family therapy with Central American war refugee families. *Journal of Strategic and Systemic Therapies, 8,* 28-35.

Arthur, N. (1995). International training: The new realities of doing business internationally. *Association of Canadian Community Colleges Community, 8.*

Arthur, N. (1997). Counselling issues with international students. *Canadian Journal of Counselling, 31,* 259-274.

Arthur, N. (1998a). Intergenerational conflict in career and life planning. In H. Suzin (ed.), *National Consultation on Career Development – 24,* 95-104. Toronto, ON: OISE Press.

Arthur, N. (1998b). Counsellor education for diversity: Where do we go from here? *Canadian Journal of Counselling, 32,* 88-103.

Arthur, N. (1998c). Using critical incidents to investigate cross-cultural transitions. Manuscript submitted for publication.

Arthur, N. & Ramaliu, A. (in press). Crisis intervention with survivors of torture. *Crisis Intervention and Time Limited Treatment.*

Austin, C. (1986). *Cross-cultural re-entry: A book of readings.* Abilene, TX: Abilene Christian University Press.

Baptiste, D. (1990). The treatment of adolescents and their families in cultural transition: Issues and recommendations. *Contemporary Family Therapy, 12*(1), 3-22.

Baptiste, D. (1993). Immigrant families, adolescents and acculturation: Insights for therapists. *Marriage and Family Review, 19*, 341-363.
Bemak, F., Chung, R. C. & Bornemann, T. H. (1996). Counseling and psychotherapy with refugees. In P. Pedersen & W. Lonner (Eds.), *Counseling across cultures* (pp. 243-263). Thousand Oaks, CA: Sage.
Berry, J. W. (1984). Multicultural policy in Canada: A social psychological analysis. *Canadian Journal of Behavioral Science, 16*, 353-370.
Berry, J. W. (1992). Acculturation and adaptation in a new society. *International Migration, 30*, 69-85.
Berry, J. W. (1997). Immigration, acculturation, and adaptation. *Applied Psychology: An International Review, 46*(1), 5-68.
Berry, J. W. & Kim, U. (1988). Acculturation and mental health. In P. R. Dasen, J. W. Berry & N. Sartorius (Eds.), *Health and cross-cultural psychology: Towards applications* (pp. 207-238). Newbury Park, CA: Sage.
Berry, J. W., Kim, U., Mindle, T. & Mok, D. (1987). Comparative studies of acculturative stress. *International Migration Review, 21*, 491-511.
Brabant, S., Palmer, C. E. & Gramling, R. (1990). Returning home: An empirical investigation of cross-cultural reentry. *International Journal of Intercultural Relations, 14*, 387-404.
Brislin, R. & Yoshida, T. (1994). Individualism and collectivism as a source of many specific cultural differences. In R. Brislin & T. Yoshida (Eds.), *Improving intercultural interactions* (pp. 71-88). Thousand Oaks, CA: Sage.
Brookfield, S. (1995). *Becoming a critically reflective teacher*. San Francisco: Jossey-Bass.
Bull, L. (1991). Indian residential schooling: The Native perspective. *Canadian Journal of Native Education, 18*, 3-63.
Church, A. T. (1982). Sojourner adjustment. *Psychological Bulletin, 91*, 540-572.
Crano S. L. & Crano, W. D. (1993). A measure of adjustment strain in international students. *Journal of Cross-Cultural Psychology, 24*, 267-283.
Cushner, K. & Nieman, C. (1997). Managing international and intercultural programs. In K. Cushner & R. W. Brislin (Ed.), *Improving intercultural interactions: Modules for cross-cultural training programs Volume 2* (pp. 129-148). Thousand Oaks, CA: Sage.
Daniels, J. & D'Andrea, M. (1996). MCT theory and ethnocentrism in counseling. In D. W. Sue, A. Ivey & P. Pedersen (Eds.), *A theory of multicultural counselling and therapy* (pp. 155-174). Pacific Grove, CA: Brooks/Cole.
Dei, G. J. (1992). *The social reality of international post-secondary students in Canada*. Ottawa: Canadian Bureau for International Education.
Esses, V. M. & Gardner, R. C. (1996). Multiculturalism in Canada: Context and current status. *Canadian Journal of Behavioural Science, 28*(3), 145-152.
France, M. H. (1997). First Nations: Helping and learning in the Aboriginal community. *Guidance and Counselling, 12*(2), 3-8.
France, M. H. & McCormick, R. (1997). Theme editorial: First Nations counselling. *Guidance and Counselling, 12*(2), 1-2.
Furnham, A. & Bochner, S. (1986). *Culture shock: Psychological reactions to unfamiliar environments*. London: Methuen.

Goodman, N. (1994). Cross-cultural training for the global executive. In R. Brislin & T. Yoshida (Eds.), *Improving intercultural interactions: Models for cross-cultural training programs* (pp. 34-54). Thousand Oaks, CA: Sage.

Granrose, C. S. & Oskamp, S. (1997). Cross-cultural work groups: An overview. In C. S. Granrose & S. Oskamp (Eds.), *Cross-cultural work groups* (pp. 1-16). Thousand Oaks, CA: Sage.

Green, H. (1997). "May I walk in beauty": First Nations and self-esteem. *Guidance and Counselling, 12*(2), 22-26.

Grieger, I. & Ponterotto, J. G. (1995). A framework for assessment in multicultural counseling. In J. G. Ponterotto, J. M. Casas, L. A. Suzuki & C. M. Alexander (Eds.), *Handbook of multicultural counseling* (pp. 357-374). Thousand Oaks, CA: Sage.

Gullahorn, J. T. & Gullahorn, J. E. (1963). An extension of the U-curve hypothesis. *Journal of Social Issues, 14*, 33-47.

Harrison, J. K., Chadwick, M. & Scales, M. (1996). The relationship between cross-cultural adjustment and the personality variables of self-efficacy and self-monitoring. *International Journal of Intercultural Relations, 20*, 167-188.

Harvey, M. G. (1997). "Inpatriation" training: The next challenge for international human resource management. *International Journal of Intercultural Relations, 21*, 393-428.

Hayes, R. L. & Lin, H. (1994). Coming to America: Developing social support systems for international students. *Journal of Multicultural Counseling and Development, 22*, 7-16.

Herr, E. L. (1993). Contexts and influences on the need for personal flexibility for the 21st century, part I. *Canadian Journal of Counselling, 27*, 148-164.

Herring, R. C. (1996). Synergetic counseling and Native American Indian students. *Journal of Counseling & Development, 74*, 542-547.

Hofstede, G. (1980). *Cultural consequences: National differences in thinking and organizing.* Beverly Hills, CA: Sage.

Indian and Northern Affairs. (1996). *Royal commission report on Aboriginal peoples 1996.* Ottawa, ON: Canada Communication Group

Indian and Northern Affairs. (1998). *Gathering strength: Canada's Aboriginal action plan.* Ottawa, ON: Government of Canada.

Ishiyama, F. I. (1995). Culturally dislocated clients: Self-validation and cultural conflict issues and counselling implications. *Canadian Journal of Counselling, 29*, 262-275.

Kealey, D. J. & Protheroe, D. R. (1996). The effectiveness of cross-cultural training for expatriates: An assessment of the literature on the issue. *International Journal of Intercultural Relations, 20*, 141-167.

Knight, J. (1994). *Internationalization: Elements and checkpoints.* CBIE Research, 7, 1-15.

Kopala, M., Esquivel, G. & Baptiste, L. (1994). Counseling approaches for immigrant children: Facilitating the acculturative process. *The School Counselor, 41*, 352-359.

Laframboise, T. D., Heyle, A. M. & Ozer, E. J. (1990). Changing and diverse roles of women in American Indian cultures. *Sex Roles, 2*, 455-476.

Lazarus, R. S. (1997). Acculturation isn't everything. *Applied Psychology: An International Review, 46*(1), 39-43.

Lazarus, R. & Folkman, S. (1984). *Stress, appraisal, and coping.* New York: Springer.

Leung, S. A. (1995). Career development and counseling: A multicultural perspective. In J. G. Ponterotto, J. M. Casas, L. A. Suzuki & C. M. Alexander (Eds.), *Handbook of multicultural counseling* (pp. 549-566). Thousand Oaks, CA: Sage.

Lysgaard, S. (1955). Adjustment in a foreign society: Norwegian Fulbright grantees visiting the United States. *International Social Science Bulletin, 10,* 45-51.

Mallinckrodt, B. & Leong, F. T. (1992). International graduate students, stress, and social support. *Journal of College Student Development, 33,* 71-78.

Martin, J. N. (1984). The intercultural reentry: Conceptualization and directions for future research. *International Journal of Intercultural Relations, 8,* 115-134.

Martin, J. N. (1986). Communication in the intercultural reentry: Student sojourners' perceptions of change in reentry relationship. *International Journal of Intercultural Relations, 10,* 1-22.

McCormick, R. M. (1997). Healing through interdependence: The role of connecting in First Nations healing practices. *Canadian Journal of Counselling, 31,* 172-184.

Morrisette, P. J. (1994). The holocaust of First Nation people: Residual effects on parenting and treatment implications. *Contemporary Family Therapy, 10,* 381-392.

Oberg, K. (1960). Cultural shock: Adjustment to new cultural environments. *Practical Anthropology, 7,* 177-182.

Palmer, D. L. (1996). Determinants of Canadian attitudes toward immigration: More than just racism? *Canadian Journal of Behavioral Sciences, 28*(3), 180-192.

Parker, B. & McEvoy, G. M. (1993). Initial examination of a model of intercultural adjustment. *International Journal of Intercultural Relations, 17,* 355-379.

Parr, G., Bradley, L. & Bingi, R. (1992). Concerns and feelings of international students. *Journal of College Student Development, 33,* 20-25.

Pedersen, P. (1990). Social and psychological factors of brain drain and reentry among international students: A survey of this topic. *McGill Journal of Education, 25,* 229-243.

Pedersen, P. B. (1991). Counseling international students. *The Counseling Psychologist, 19,* 10-58.

Pederson, P. (1993). Mediating multicultural conflict by separating behaviors from expectations in a cultural grid. *International Journal of Intercultural Relations, 17,* 343-353.

Pedersen, P. (1995). The culture-bound counsellor as an unintentional racist. *Canadian Journal of Counselling, 29,* 197-205.

Pedersen, P. & Ivey, A. (1993). *Culture-centered counseling and interviewing skills: A practical guide.* London: Praeger.

Restoule, B. (1997). Providing services to Aboriginal clients. *Guidance and Counselling, 12*(2), 13-17.

Rogers, J. & Ward, C. (1993). Expectation-experience discrepancies and psychological adjustment during cross-cultural reentry. *International Journal of Intercultural Relations, 17,* 185-196.

Ross, J. & Ross, J. (1992). Keep the circle strong: Native health promotion. *Journal of Speech Language Pathology, 16,* 291-302.

Saphiere, D. (1996). Productive behaviors of global business teams. *International Journal of Intercultural Relations, 20,* 227-259.

Schlossberg, N. (1984). *Counseling adults in transition: Linking practice with theory.* New York: Springer.

Schlossberg, N. (1992). Adult development theories: Ways to illuminate the adult development experience. In H. D. Lea & Z. B. Leibowitz (Eds.), *Adult career development: Concepts, issues, and practices* (2nd Ed.), (pp. 2-16). Alexandria, VA: The National Career Development Association.

Searle, W. & Ward, C. (1990). The prediction of psychological and sociocultural adjustment during cross-cultural transitions. *International Journal of Intercultural Relations, 14,* 449-464.

Singelis, T. M. & Pedersen, P. (1997). Conflict and mediation across cultures. In K. Cushner & R. W. Brislin (Eds.), *Improving intercultural interactions: Modules for cross-cultural training programs,* Volume 2 (pp. 184-204).

Statistics Canada (1995). *Projections of visible minority population groups, Canada, provinces and regions, 1991-2016* (Statistics Canada Catalogue 91-541-XPE). Ottawa.

Strober, B. (1994). Social work interventions to alleviate Cambodian refugee psychological distress. *International Social Work, 37,* 23-35.

Sue, D. W. (1995). Multicultural organizational development: Implications for the counseling profession. In J. G. Ponterotto, J. M. Casas, L. A. Suzuki & C. M. Alexander (Eds.), *Handbook of multicultural counseling* (pp. 474-492). Thousand Oaks, CA: Sage.

Sue, D. W., Arredondo, P. & McDavis, R. J. (1992). Multicultural counseling competencies and standards: A call to the profession. *Journal of Counseling and Development, 70,* 477-486.

Sue, D. W. & Sue, D. (1990). *Counseling the culturally different.* New York: John Wiley & Sons.

Thomas, K. & Althen, G. (1989). In P. B. Pedersen, J. G. Draguns, W. J. Lonner & J. E. Trimble (Eds.), *Counseling across cultures* (3rd Ed.) (pp. 205-241). Honolulu: University of Hawaii Press.

Tiller, A. D. & Lesser, B. (1992). *International students and higher education: Canadian choices.* Ottawa: Canadian Bureau for International Education.

Tyler, A. & Boxer, D. (1996). Sexual harassment? Cross-cultural/cross-linguistic perspectives. *Discourse & Society, 7,* 107-133.

Uehara, A. (1986). The nature of American student reentry adjustment and perceptions of the sojourn experience. *International Journal of Intercultural Relations, 10,* 415-438.

Walton, S. J. (1990). Stress management training for overseas effectiveness. *International Journal of Intercultural Relations, 14,* 507-527.

Wang, M. (1997). Reentry and reverse culture shock. In K. Cushner & R. W. Brislin (Eds.), *Improving intercultural interactions: Modules for cross-cultural training programs, Vol. 2* (pp. 109-128). Thousand Oaks, CA: Sage.

Ward, C. (1996). Acculturation. In D. Landis & R. Bhaget (Eds.), *Handbook of intercultural training* (2nd Ed.). Newbury Park, CA: Sage.

Ward, C. & Kennedy, A. (1993). Where's the "culture" in cross-cultural transition? Comparative studies of sojourner adjustment. *Journal of Cross-Cultural Psychology, 24,* 221-249.

Wehrly, B. (1988). Cultural diversity from an international perspective: Part two. *Journal of Multicultural Counseling and Development, 16,* 3-15.

Westwood, M. J. & Ishiyama, F. I. (1991). Challenges in counseling immigrant clients: Understanding intercultural barriers to career adjustment. *Journal of Employment Counseling, 28,* 130-143.

Westwood, M. J., Lawrence, W. S. & Paul, D. (1986). Preparing for re-entry: A program for the sojourning student. *International Journal for the Advancement of Counselling, 9,* 221-230.

Winkelman, M. (1994). Cultural shock and adaptation. *Journal of Counseling and Development, 73,* 121-126.

Zaharna, R. S. (1989). Self-shock: The double-binding challenge of identity. *International Journal of Intercultural Relations, 13,* 501-525.

Zussman, D. & Poapst, G. (1995). *International education is a bottom line issue: A strategy for building an internationally competent workforce.* Ottawa: Canadian Bureau for International Education.

Chapter 3
Skills for Navigating Life Transitions

Bryan Hiebert

To a large extent, life can be seen as a series of transitions, frequently occurring on several different fronts at the same time. In a sense, transition is a steady state faced by most youth and adults. People are virtually always in a state of transition, moving from one life situation to another, in a context that is constantly changing. Change is not an option – it is a given. The only real question is whether to try and manage the change process or submit to being a passive recipient of fate. To successfully navigate life's transitions requires very different skill sets than were needed 20 years ago. Furthermore, because of the diversity in the transitions that people face, an extensive and diverse set of skills will be needed. The focus in this chapter is on skills that are useful for empowering young people to proactively take charge of the transition process. Initially, the process of change and an approach managing the change process are outlined. Then a framework is presented for organizing skills that help prepare youth to deal effectively with the world they will encounter. Brief descriptions of these skills are provided and follow-up references are given for readers who want more details. The chapter concludes with an outline of potential roles for other key stakeholders in the process of youth transition.

Managing Change

The Change Process

Recent studies in health behavior have shown that positive lifestyle changes have been enhanced by utilizing a model of "Stages of Change" (Prochaska, Norcross & Diclemente, 1994). As Prochaska points out, most people follow a typical pattern when they go about making changes in their lives. This pattern can be thought of as stages in the change process. Prochaska envisions five stages of change: precontemplation, contemplation, preparation, action and maintenance. Individuals typically recycle through these stages several times, and for most people, the process is not as linear as the model might appear. However, the model does provide a useful framework for understanding the change process, therefore, it is illustrated in Figure 3-1 and summarized briefly below.

Figure 3-1. Readiness For Change.

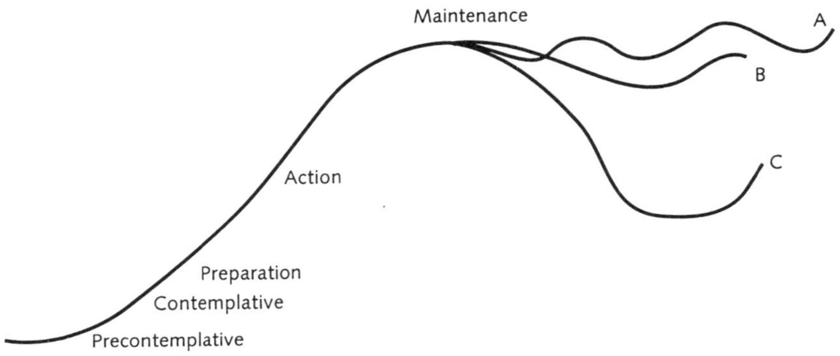

[Diagram showing a curve rising through stages: Precontemplative, Contemplative, Preparation, Action, peaking at Maintenance, then branching into three paths labeled A, B, and C.]

Precontemplation. During precontemplation there is really no intention to change in the foreseeable future. Individuals might have some awareness of the need to change, but they are not really aware of a problem. They may have a vague sense that something needs to be done, but there is no real commitment to change. Their attitude could be summed up by the statements: "I'd probably feel better if I got more exercise, but I really can't spare the time" or "I might encounter fewer problems if I was more open-minded, but other people are so opinionated that it probably wouldn't make much difference."

Contemplation. As people become more aware of the existence of a problem or the need to make change in their lives, they begin to think more seriously of attempting to make some changes. At this point they are thinking about making some changes, but typically are not yet committed to taking action. They may be intimidated by the enormity of the change or they may not know exactly how to go about making the changes they want. People often stay in this stage for a long period, experiencing discomfort and wanting to do something about it, but still not taking action. Their attitude could be summed up by the statements: "My life is crazy and unmanageable and I really think I should work on it" or "I really do need a job and I should start working at it more seriously."

Preparation. As people enter the preparation stage, they have made a decision to change, but are not fully committed to beginning the process. Instead, they go about making arrangements for all of the things that need to be done before they can begin changing. They may "need" to buy a new jogging suit before they start working out, or get all of their filing done before they begin their term paper, or see how their friends are doing before they start looking for work. Individuals in the preparation stage probably will begin to take action within the next 1-6 months, but right now they are still getting ready to do it. Their attitude could be summed up by the statements: "I know I would feel better if I ate more healthy foods, but I just bought groceries and I can't waste any of the snack food I purchased" or "I know I would feel better about myself if I just got to work on this paper, but I just can't work at a messy desk."

Action. Action is the stage where people actually begin to modify their behaviors, or change their environmental context, in order to initiate change or overcome a problem. Action involves actually making changes. It requires considerable commitment of time and energy and is most successful when approached in a systematic manner. The attitude of people in the action stage could be summed up by the statements: "I am committed to reduce the stress levels in my life and will set aside 20 minutes every day to do Transcendental Meditation" or "I really want to raise my grades and starting today I'm going to schedule 2 hours every evening to review my notes. I'm going to do it first, before I phone any of my friends."

Maintenance. When people have accomplished their change goals, they need to work at preventing relapse. Making sure that changes last more than one day is really a continuation of the change process and maintaining change is not automatic. For some behaviors, it may require a lifetime of attention to keep the change within reasonable limits. During maintenance, people's attitude could be summed up by the statements: "I going to keep coming to aerobics class to reinforce the progress I have already made" or "I'm going to put a reminder on the door of my room to say something nice to each of my parents every day so that I continue to get along with them better."

As Figure 3-1 depicts, the process of change is gradual during the initial stages of the change process and very little change is taking place. However, as a person moves into the preparation and action stages, more rapid progress is made and the change is more evident. After change goals have been met, people enter a maintenance period, where they attempt, with varying degrees of success, to make sure the changes endure.

The Maintenance Stage can take several forms. The most typical pattern is the stable pattern depicted by "Path A" in Figure 3-1. People oscillate back and forth, sometimes being a bit more successful, sometimes a bit less, but more-or-less steady at their desired level of change. These people realize that maintaining a change requires a lifetime of management. They keep an eye on how they are doing, they set some boundaries around how far they are willing to let things slide, and when they see themselves slipping close to those boundaries, they take action to get themselves back on track.

For other people, the maintenance process looks more like Path B. They rejoice in their achievement, become complacent about the focused efforts they used to achieve their goal, and begin to drift back towards where they were in the beginning. Most often, these people catch themselves drifting from their goal, and re-introduce the focused effort they used to achieve their previous accomplishment. They move themselves back to action and bring themselves back to their desired level.

For others, the maintenance process looks more like Path C. They tend to say to themselves "Well, I've done it, now I can just take it easy." They make the mistake of thinking that the new level is permanent and will not require any further effort. In reality, the task of replacing many years of undesirable habit is a never ending process. As soon as people let down their guard, the old habits begin to resurface. However, even in this case, all is not lost. It is simply a matter of re-entering the process of change, moving rapidly through the initial stages of the change process, re-committing to the change and taking action in the same manner that helped them achieve their goal initially.

There are many factors influencing whether the maintenance process will look more like Path A or B or C. Generally speaking, when people use a purposeful and systematic approach to taking action or maintaining change, they are more successful. They also end up feeling more optimistic about their ability to manage the change process. The next section describes some guiding principles that have demonstrated success in helping people take charge of the process of making changes in their lives.

Being an Active Agent in the Change Process

People often resolve to make changes in their lives, develop new skills or alter old habits. In most cases, the primary "tool" used to accomplish this change is willpower: People make up their minds to do something and then try to make it happen. Sometimes willpower is sufficient to produce change, however in many cases willpower breaks down, change does not occur and people end up feeling frustrated. In these cases willpower was not enough. People's lists of unrealized New Year's Resolutions is testimony to the fact that many people need additional skills or approaches in order to increase their chances of being able to meet their goals. "Self-management" is the term used in the psychological literature to describe such procedures.

Self-management procedures were developed for the purpose of helping people accomplish the goals they set for themselves. They are particularly important for people who are in the action and maintenance stages described earlier in this chapter. When people have methods for taking action to make changes in their lives that work in a reliable manner, they tend to feel more in charge of their life. They feel more like an active agent in their experience, rather than a passive recipient of what fate hands out. The concept "personal agency" was formulated to describe people who have the belief that they are able to play a large part in their life experience. When people set out to make changes in their lives, a few simple self-management tips can help them increase the chances of success. Typically, self-management skills are clustered into four basic steps (Bandura, 1995, 1997; Kanfer & Gaelick-Buys, 1991, Martin & Martin, 1983).

Goal setting. Research has shown that people who set specific, incremental and realistic goals accomplish their goals more frequently and accomplish higher goals (see Rice, 1992, for a summary.) Specific goals are met more often than vague goals. Usually, the more specific a goal is, the greater the chance of the goal being reached. Vague goals are seldom met because there are no definite benchmarks of success. Without tangible indicators of success, people have difficulty gauging their progress towards their goals. Generally speaking, specific goals are observable. They pass the third person test, i.e., someone who didn't know what the goal was, could observe whether or not the goal had been reached. Thus, specific goals often have numbers, time lines, amounts, and definite observable behaviors attached to them. The vague goal, "I'm going to be more understanding," is less likely to be accomplished than the more specific goal, "I'm going to say at least one nice thing to every person I work with each day next week."

Incremental goals are more readily accomplished than "all-or-nothing" goals. When people take one large goal and divide it up into several smaller goals, they are more likely to accomplish the large goal. Thus, the goal of "becoming more fit" is more likely to be accomplished if it is broken down into several sub-goals, e.g., walk for 20 minutes three times next week (on Sunday, Tuesday, and Friday), four times the week after, and five times on the third week. Breaking down a large goal into smaller goals gives people many opportunities to experience success, rather than one all-or-nothing chance to be successful. Having many sequential goals also makes it easier for people to see the progress they are making towards the end point. Being able to gauge progress is more encouraging and helps people accomplish their goals more easily.

People are more likely to accomplish goals that are realistic, rather than too high. All too often people set their sights higher than it is physically possible to attain. The attitude often appears to be "I never quite meet my goal, so I'll aim higher, and try to reach the higher goal, then when I don't reach it, I'll end up where I really wanted to be in the first place." Such an attitude most often represents a planned failure experience. The person sets off knowing full well that the goal will not be met. When the target change is realistic, and the goal is well-incremented, each incremental step is specifically stated, and some tangible evidence that the step has been accomplished is in place, then people are placed in a situation where success is more probable and goal attainment is most often easier.

Charting progress. People who self-monitor their attempts to change and chart their progress more often reach their goals. The type of chart is not crucial as long as each incremental goal is clearly observable on the chart. Appropriate charting methods could include: a thermometer such as those used in fund raising campaigns, a photocopy of the table of contents of a term paper with the completed portions checked off, or a line graph indicating weight or number of workouts per week. All of these represent useful and appropriate ways to use charting. The chart should be placed in a prominent position where it can be a frequent reminder of how successful a person is being (i.e., the number of incremental goals that have been completed).

Some people find that making a commitment with someone else (or themselves) can help them achieve their goals. The type of contract is less important than the commitment that it contains.

Potential areas where a contract could be useful in helping people meet goals include situations such as: observing an in-class practice of group discussion skills, exercising at a regular time, reducing caffeine consumption, telephoning once a week to ask if the weekly goal has been met, or waiting until the target end goal has been met before buying a new sweater. This type of contracting usually helps people achieve their goal, especially if the contracts are specific with respect to contingencies involved: who will do what, when and to what extent.

Evaluating progress. People are almost always evaluating what they do, but often the way they evaluate does not help them achieve their goals. Research has shown (Kanfer & Gaelick-Buys, 1991; Mahoney & Thoresen, 1974) that people who use objective information to evaluate progress towards goals usually achieve their goals more frequently. The best way to evaluate progress is by comparing the self-monitoring data that is being used to chart progress to the specific criteria listed in the goal statements. When goals are specific and observable, and a process is created to track and chart progress, then people tend to stay focused on their successes and this in turn helps keep them motivated and making progress.

Self-praise. People who reward themselves for their accomplishments usually achieve their goals more easily and more frequently. The rewards can range from verbal self-praise, "Hey, you did it, I knew you could, I'm proud of you for that" or "I did it, I knew I could, I'm proud of myself for that," to specific concrete material rewards, such as going to a movie, buying a new sweater, going for a walk. The important thing is that receiving the reward is contingent on achieving the goal. People who do this type of self-rewarding for goals achieved, achieve their goals more often.

Finally, it is important to say a word about commitment. The story is told of a chicken and a pig walking down the street together. They see a sign that reads "Bacon and eggs for breakfast, $3.99." The chicken says "Hey, look at that. They're giving us double billing for breakfast." The pig replies "Sure, it's easy for you to say. All it requires from you is a contribution. For me it's total commitment." Commitment is probably the most necessary requirement for people to make changes in their lives. People who do not really want to reach a goal will not reach it regardless of how much goal setting, charting, contracting and self-praising is done. They will remain in precontemplation forever. But for people who genuinely wish to make changes, the self-management procedures described above usually assist in achieving more and higher goals, more frequently, and with fewer adverse and frustrating side effects.

Life Skills for Dealing Successfully with Transitions

Given the rapidly changing context in which people live today and the broad range of demands that all people, and young people in particular, face, it is important to have a broad range of skills with from which to draw. People with meager coping skill repertoires are more likely to encounter situations which they lack the necessary resources to handle successfully. Conversely, people with a larger repertoire of skills and talents are more likely to be able to deal with the multitude and complexity of issues they face. For people with more extensive skill repertoires, the process of initiating, and sustaining change will be easier and the probability of success will be greater. The remainder of this chapter is devoted to outlining some of the specific skills that can be used to deal successfully with high frequency demands that young people face.

Personal Vision for Life: A Starting Point

Many young people, and a surprising number of adults as well, have difficulty initiating and sustaining personal change because they do not have a clear sense of what they want to get out of their lives. They lack a basic understanding of who they are and where they want to go with their lives. Thus, when barriers are encountered, and it is inevitable that people will encounter barriers, they are thrown off course and have difficulty getting back on track. Without a personal vision, there is no beacon to guide their day-by-day practice and they become unduly influenced by the multitude of daily hassles they encounter. If they had a personal vision for their life, when they were finishing dealing with the unexpected barriers that arise, they would be able to regain direction, and continue with their quest.

Vision statements are short, easily remembered phrases that sum up what an organization, or person, is striving for. A vision statement encapsulates the *"raison d'etre"* for an organization or a person. "Every child a wanted child" is a suitable beacon for the National Planned Parenthood Association. "We try harder" is a suitable vision for a firm that is second place and may well catapult it into top spot. However, in spite of the fact that most businesses are beginning to realize the importance of a clear vision, few individuals have developed a clear sense of what their lives are all about.

Many educators have found that a few simple experiential exercises can help people establish a sense of personal vision. Sometimes it is useful to ask people to think about an epitaph for their own personal tombstone. This is the phase they would like to be remembered by. Alternatively, they might be asked to write an obituary, describing how they would like to be remembered after they die, and then to encapsulate it in a short, easily-remembered statement. After that, ask them to lay out a plan for making sure that the epitaph is obvious to the people they interact with: What is their 5-year plan that will lead them on their way to their life vision? What is the 3-month plan that will move them towards that goal, and what will they do tomorrow that takes them one step in the same direction? Such exercises often help people get in touch with the inner self that longs for fulfillment, with the passion that drives their soul. What is the sense of managing transition if there is no direction to the life journey?

However, care must be taken when developing a vision for life to realize that it must not be a "written in stone" exercise. People's goals for living change from time to time. Noer (1993) encourages people to avoid being a tap root tree where there is a single source that provides all our emotional, social, psychological and physical sustenance. Diffusing our root system, so that we can draw sustenance from multiple sources for meaning, social life, learning, professional development and community means that all of our eggs are not in one basket and that we have multiple resources at our beck and call. As Tocher (1998) so aptly points out, our vision for life needs to be a beacon that remains open to change, sensitive to the "herald of adventure" that invites us to new horizons and puts us in touch with the inner self that longs for fulfillment (p. 74). It is important to have some direction, for it provides purpose for living, but it also is important to remain open to new experiences and sensitive to new opportunities.

Self-Concept: A Central Motivating Factor

Self-concept literally refers to people's sense, or concept, of themselves and it is at the heart of their vision for living. Self-concept is multifaceted, incorporating the multitude of roles in which a person participates: student, son, daughter, friend, parent, jogger, church member, worker or volunteer. All of the roles in which a person is engaged form part of the person's "sense of self," or their self-concept. Self-esteem refers to the degree of positiveness inherent in the person's self-concept and plays an important role in people's experiences. Self-esteem stems primarily from two sources: people's thoughts (and feelings) about their ability to do something and their thoughts (and feelings) about the outcomes of their efforts. People who don't have a very positive image of themselves tend to think poorly of their ability to deal with the situations they encounter and tend to think that even if they do attempt a task it will not result in something that is worthwhile. This poor view of their ability to handle a situation can trigger a stressful reaction even in relatively low-key situations and can be instrumental in precipitating a failure situation.

The work of Bandura and his students (cf. Bandura, 1995, 1997) provides some insight into the way self-esteem works to influence people's life goals. Bandura introduced the term "self-efficacy" to refer to people's beliefs that they are able to accomplish certain tasks. People with high self-efficacy regarding a particular task believe that they are able to perform that task successfully. Efficacy expectations refer to the outcomes that people expect to occur upon successful completion of the task. As Martin and Martin (1983) point out, when people believe that they can perform a task successfully, and believe that the task is worthwhile, motivation typically is high. Thus, people with a high degree of self-efficacy tend to be highly motivated, tend to believe that they will be successful in the tasks they undertake, and generally are more likely to believe they are active agents in creating their futures. This concept has come to be know as "personal agency" and will be dealt with in more detail later in this chapter.

Self-esteem is greatly influenced by the number of success experiences a person has. People who have a lot of failure experiences, and are told repeatedly that they are likely to fail, usually begin to believe that they have little ability and are unlikely to succeed. Their self-talk usually will be negative and their self-coaching usually will prompt them to fail. On the other hand, people who have a greater number of success experiences, and are reminded frequently that they have ability and are likely to succeed, usually begin to believe in their ability and see themselves as successful. These people typically give themselves encouragement, tell themselves that they can perform certain tasks and that the results of their efforts will be successful, and as a result, their self-esteem is high.

Most programs to build self-esteem have two main components: an action plan that is designed to foster success and a plan for managing self-talk that prompts a person to follow the action plan and maintain a positive focus. Parents and teachers need to structure the experiences in which young people engage in order to ensure a high proportion of success experiences. This does not mean avoiding challenges and it involves more than engaging in "feel good activities," a perspective which seems to have invaded some educational circles. It is a planned program to help shape a child's development. Typically, such programs incorporate basic self-management strategies that involve setting goals that are realistic, achievable, incremental, gradual and observable. Usually there is some form of charting or record keeping to help keep the focus on success. For some people, contracting helps them stay focused on their goals. For most people, some explicit acknowledgment of their accomplishments also helps them keep focused on their success experiences. This acknowledgment can take the form of external rewards, but increasingly, people are finding that simply telling themselves that they have been successful and that they are happy with their own accomplishments can be a powerful motivator.

People with low self-esteem are known to have very negative self-talk patterns. They habitually put themselves down, think of themselves as losers, expect failure when they undertake difficult tasks, and beat up on themselves for making mistakes. Thus, most programs to increase self-esteem have a component that is aimed at helping people change their self-talk habits so they are more self-supportive and self-encouraging. I often point out to people that on any given day they spend more time with themselves than they spend with anyone else. If the person you spend most of your time with is constantly hassling you, telling you how you'll likely mess up, how you are such a loser, how you've never been any good at anything, then you are likely to end up feeling put down and unmotivated, perhaps even depressed and stressed. On the other hand, if the person you spend most of your time with is giving you encouragement, telling you how hard you are trying, reminding you that you are doing your best, then you are likely to be more motivated, accomplish more and feel less stressed as well. The goal of the self-talk component of programs to build self-esteem is to help people talk to themselves in a way that is supportive and encouraging. It is a matter of creating self-statements that focus on the things a person can do (rather than the things they have trouble with) and the successful experiences they have (rather than the discouragements).

One simple procedure that can be used to promote this positive self-dialogue might be called a "+/- card." Divide a small index card in half, marking one side "+" and the other side "-". Each time you say something to yourself (or think a thought about yourself) place a check mark on the card. Place it on the "+" side if the thought is positive, self-supportive or encouraging, and on the "-" side if the thought is negative, critical or a put-down. After counting thoughts for a couple of days to see what your typical pattern is, set a goal of increasing the number of check marks on the "+" side. As the "+" side increases the "-" side typically will automatically go down. Most people notice that positive and negative comments do not have the same impact. In fact, one negative can often undo four or five positive comments. This means that the goal is to produce about five times as many positives as there are negatives, in order that the overall balance will favor of the positive side. This is sometimes referred to as the "1-to-5 rule." Sometimes people find that posting positive reminders in strategic places helps them maintain their positive focus and reminds them to be encouraging to themselves. Most people find that after two or three weeks, the process of talking positively to themselves is becoming more natural. Then they can phase out the recording card. Research studies with numerous client groups in a wide variety of contexts, ranging from college students, to learning disabled adolescents, to at-risk youth, suggest that this sort of approach has a predictable impact in helping people use their self-talk as an ally in helping them achieve the goals they want in life (Bandura, 1995, 1997; Davey Baustad, in press; Hiebert & Malcolm, 1988; Hutchinson, 1995; Schlichter, 1978).

One caution should be mentioned when developing school-based programs to raise self-esteem. Research by my colleagues and I in six high schools and one junior high (Collins & Hiebert, 1995; Collins & Angen, 1997; Hiebert, Collins & Cairns, 1994; Hiebert, Kemeny & Kurchak in press; Reeh, Hiebert & Cairns, 1998) suggests that although parents think that many adolescents have self-esteem problems, students do not see "lack of self-esteem" as a high priority need. Thus, programs to increase self-esteem likely need to contain both general elements and components targeted at specific people. For example, a program to increase the number of success experiences and to focus on people's successes and celebrate people's accomplishments likely would be of benefit to all young people, as would programs aimed generally at helping people manage their self-talk so that it is more self supportive and encouraging (see Davey Baustad, in press; Lessard, in press; Mailandt, in press.) However, some young people, especially those with a history of failure experiences and an environment of psychological abuse, might require special attention and a systematic program especially tailored to their own individual needs in order to begin the process of rebuilding their self-esteem.

Personal Agency:
Being an Active Agent in One's Destiny

When developing programs for young people aimed at fostering a sense that they are active agents in their lives, it is important to proceed from the bottom up, focusing on input from the young people themselves. Research conducted by my colleagues and myself has discovered important differences in the perceptions of adults and students (see Collins & Hiebert, 1995; Collins & Angen, 1997; Hiebert, Collins & Cairns, 1994; Hiebert, Kemeny & Kurchak in press; Reeh, Hiebert & Cairns, 1998.) These findings have been replicated in six high schools and one junior high school. Parents and school personnel tended to be problem-focused in their perceptions of adolescent needs. They saw adolescents as having problems with interpersonal relationships, peer pressure and low self-esteem. In addition, school personnel saw students as having difficulties interacting with their parents and parents saw their children as having difficulty dealing with teachers. Students on the other hand tended to be more solution-focused in their own self-reports. They saw themselves as benefiting from some training in interpersonal communication in order to get along better with their peers, parents and teachers. They wanted to have more career counselling. They thought they would benefit by learning some problem-solving skills. They expressed pressure associated with academic demands and wanted the skills to be able to do well in school. They saw their parents as generally being supportive (student ratings of parent support were higher than parent perceptions of the support they offered). Similarly, student reports of their relationship with teachers was more positive than teachers thought it would be. Generally speaking, the data we have collected to date paint a positive picture of young people, who are aware of the problems they face and are wanting to be better equipped to deal with those problems.

Therefore, in order to provide youth with the skills they need to navigate successfully through the educational system and to experience success with the transition from schooling to the labor force, it will be important to look at the high frequency demands that young people face and to create a forum where they can learn the skills needed to deal successfully with these demands. It becomes a challenge to all adults to help young people acquire the skills needed to deal successfully with the future they are experiencing every day.

Skills for dealing with career transitions

Career-related concerns are one of the most frequently reported worries of young people (Allen & Hiebert, 1991; Collins & Hiebert, 1995; Hiebert et al., 1994; Posterski & Bibby, 1988). In helping youth achieve the skills they need to be successful in the workplace, it is important that a contemporary framework be adopted. The "High 5 (+1)" which was outlined in Chapter 1 provides a starting point, however, more specifics are needed in order to build a solid skill set that will be useful in today's labor market.

Recently, the Conference Board of Canada has published an Employability Skills Profile (see McLaughlin, 1995). This is a list of skills, identified by employers, that people need in order to function effectively in the work place. The skills are clustered into three groups: academic skills, personal management skills and teamwork skills. The academic skills include: basic literacy and numeracy, but also the ability to communicate effectively, think critically, problem solve, access information sources and an attitude of life long learning. The personal management skills include: a positive attitude, willingness to accept responsibility, initiative, integrity, self-directedness, confidence, self-esteem, ability to plan and manage time and money, and adaptability. Teamwork skills include the ability to: work with others, understand and contribute to the organization's goals, respect the thoughts and opinions of others in a group, and exercise "give and take" to achieve group results. This is a very different skill set than was required for success in the past. Traditional academic skills are less prominent, as are technical skills. Employers are saying that they can train for the job-specific skills, but have trouble training for the team work and personal management skills. This is not to say that traditional academic skills are not important; they are, but they are also not enough. Increasingly, firms are acknowledging the importance of the academic skills, but focus more on the personal skills when making hiring decisions, and even more so, in making decisions about whether or not to fire an employee.

Amundson and Borgen (Amundson, Borgen & Tench, 1995; Borgen & Amundson, 1995) extend this theme. They point out that the new labor market reality that youth face is characterized by downsizing, fewer middle-management positions, increasing worker responsibilities, increasing accountability, increasing part-time work and more contracting out. There is an increased emphasis on customer service, necessitating better marketing, managing all aspects of a customer's experience and greater emphasis on interpersonal relationships, both between workers and customers and also between workers and co-workers. To succeed in this environment requires a planful and purposeful attitude, skills for exploring possibilities and options, strategies for developing multiple career plans, the ability to market and be an advocate for oneself, and personal coping skills to deal with stress, manage anger and so forth. To help foster the development of these diverse skill sets, teachers, counsellors and parents will need a different and more extensive set of skills and knowledge, an attitude that acknowledges the importance of maintaining current information, and a process for acquiring and updating information (because of the rapidly changing nature of that information). The skills identified by the Conference Board of Canada and Borgen and Amundson and Borgen can be thought of as way to help people feel empowered about their career paths.

Skills for dealing with stress

Young people report substantial amounts of stress, suggesting that they are often in situations where they feel overtaxed. For example, Allen and Hiebert (1991) found that the mean frequency of stress-related symptoms reported by high school students was equal to or higher than the norms for adult psychiatric outpatients. Similarly, mean scores for both transitory and chronic anxiety were higher for the sample of adolescents than the norms for college students or adults. This replicated an earlier observation, made while field testing a relaxation program with grade 12 students (Hiebert & Eby, 1985), that the frequency of stress-related symptoms and state and trait anxiety scores were higher for the students than for teachers. Contrary to the common myth that "young people never had it so good," it would seem that many young people are having difficulty coping with the demands they are facing.

The main reason for the high rates of stress among youth is that they simply have not developed the skills needed to handle the demands they are facing. Most researchers (cf. Hiebert, 1988, 1991; Lazarus & Folkman, 1984; Rice, 1992) agree that stress does not come from the demands people face per se. Stress comes from people's perception that they do not have the resources for dealing satisfactorily with the demands they are facing. When addressing stress and youth, it is important to realize that it is the perception of an individual young person that determines the degree of stress being experienced. It is the young person's perception of the nature and intensity of the demands being faced, the young person's perception of his or her coping capability, and the young person's perception of the consequences likely to occur in the situation, that will determine the amount of stress the young person experiences.

Research with young people supports the theoretical observations described above. For example, in an extensive investigation of adolescent coping, Compas and colleagues (Compas, 1987; Compas, Malcarne & Fondacaro, 1988) found that adolescents who were more adept at generating problem-focused coping alternatives experienced fewer adjustment problems. In a similar vein, Allen and Hiebert (1991) found that students with fewer coping resources reported higher levels of stress and more stress-related symptoms. Arthur and Hiebert (1996) found that post-secondary students had few back up resources to draw on if their typical way of dealing with a situation was not being successful. Further, Hiebert, Kirby and Jeknavorian (1989) found that generally speaking adolescents had rather meager coping repertoires. These observations combine to underscore the importance of addressing stress control with young people.

In trying to control stress there are a number of common sense things that people can do to reduce stress that also have documented support in the literature. These include: sleep, exercise, nutrition and social support. I refer to these as "common SENSS approaches to stress control." Getting enough sleep is an important part of control stress. Most people have observed that on days when they are well rested, they have a greater capacity for dealing with the minor trials and tribulations they encounter. Being well-rested is especially important in periods of high demand. When the demands are increasing, it should be a signal to get the proper amount of rest, rather than rob one's self of sleep in order to try and get more done.

Regular exercise helps to control stress in several ways. Exercise helps people reduce the level of stress hormones in the blood stream and often produces a mental tranquillity similar to meditation. This effect helps many people regain equilibrium after being stressed. Further, when people exercise regularly it improves their aerobic functioning, which in turn helps them recover from stress more rapidly. Recent studies suggest that it is not necessary to be an exercise fanatic and that moderate exercise, if it is regular, can be accompanied by substantial reductions in stress and gains in fitness (Baydala, Malec & Hiebert, 1997; Malec & Hiebert, 1997).

Nutrition can have a large impact on people's susceptibility to stress. The effects of caffeine on inducing and sustaining arousal, and refined sugar in retarding recovery time when people are stressed, are well documented (see Greenberg, 1990; Mason, 1980).

The most common sources of caffeine in Western diets are coffee, chocolate and cola beverages. Chocolate bars, and coffee with sugar in it, create a double effect by combining caffeine and refined sugar: the caffeine helps get people worked up and the sugar helps keep them worked up. Often people feel worked up and jittery simply because they have had too much caffeine. Reducing the intake of caffeine and refined sugar can have a powerful calming effect and leave people better able to cope with the demands they face. On the other hand, people with inadequate amounts of Vitamin B in their diets tend to have reduced recovery time when they are stressed. Vitamin B is utilized in helping people return to normal after they have been stressed. Sometimes, people who experience frequent stressors have depleted stores of Vitamin B. As a result they recover from stress more slowly than they usually would. Eating vegetables rich in Vitamin B (broccoli, asparagus, peas, spinach, mushrooms, corn) or taking a daily Vitamin B supplement will make sure that Vitamin B levels are adequate and stress recovery time is not prolonged.

Finally, social support has demonstrated a powerful buffering effect for adults experiencing stress (Billings & Moos, 1981; House, 1981; Lazarus & Folkman, 1984). People who have a strong social support network are far less likely to be overtaxed by the demands they face. The size and composition of the support group and how often or where it meets does not seem to be important. The fact that support is available seems to be the central ingredient for reducing stress. Having one or more friends that a person can turn to for a pat on the back or a word of comfort in times of trouble seems to help reduce the potential for being overwhelmed by the demands one faces. The key to providing social support is to avoid giving advice and instead to listen to the concern in a way that demonstrates that the person has been understood.

For cases where a more comprehensive approach is needed, Hiebert (1988, 1991) has developed a useful model. The model approaches stress control from two directions. **Stressor management** focuses on controlling stress by seeking to reduce the imbalance between the demands people face and their resources for dealing with those demands. This is accomplished by reducing the demands or increasing the resources for dealing with the demands. **Stress management** focuses on controlling stress by helping people feel more calm in situations which they find stressful. This is accomplished by teaching people skills that help to reduce their physiological, cognitive and/or behavioral responses to being overtaxed. The model is depicted in Figure 3-2 and described briefly below with examples of how to approach stress control from a contemporary and comprehensive perspective.

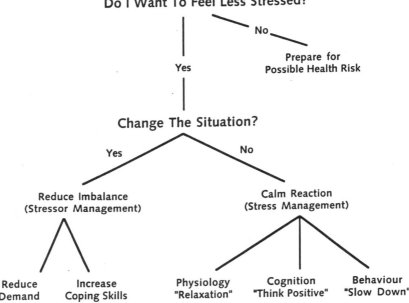

Figure 3-2. A Comprehensive Model for Stress Control

The process of controlling stress begins by exploring ways to manage the demands that are being faced to see if they can be made more reasonable. There is an old saying: "If you have a sliver in your finger try to pull it out before you enroll in a pain control course." The same is true when trying to reduce stress – first, explore ways to **reduce or change demands** so they are more manageable. Sometimes it is possible to do things like: arrange work schedules so it is not necessary to drive in rush hour traffic, negotiate a different assignment in a course, get help with a special project, change duties with a colleague so your part of a project is one which you have better skills to handle, increase lighting in your work space, or have sound barriers or special air filters installed to reduce the impact of environmental demands. Sometimes students who experience exam stress simply register in courses with no exams and people with public speaking anxiety do not take on responsibilities that involve addressing large groups of people. All of the above examples illustrate how people can reduce or change some of the demands they face and reduce the possibility that the demands will overtax them.

In cases where the demands are outside of a person's control, or where attempting to alter the demands is not feasible, the next step in a comprehensive stress control program is to explore ways of dealing with the demand more effectively. Sometimes it is possible to get help dealing with demands. For example, work tasks can be delegated or temporary help sometimes can be hired at peak times. In other cases, it is possible to learn new skills to handle stressful situations more effectively. People who experience public speaking stress often reduce their stress by enrolling in a public speaking course or joining Toastmasters. People who experience a lot of time pressure find the pressure goes down when they learn better time management skills. New teachers often find that when they learn better skills for developing a cooperative learning environment in their classrooms (classroom management skills), stress associated with student misbehavior declines. Parents often find that when they learn more effective parenting skills, they experience child rearing as less stressful. The list of appropriate skill training emphases is extensive and depends on the nature of the demands being faced. The list potentially could include: budgeting to help deal with financial stressors, communication skills to deal with interpersonal stress, conflict resolution skills for dealing with interpersonal hassles, assertiveness training to avoid stress associated with dealing with demanding or unreasonable people, study skills for dealing with academic stress, exam writing skills, job search programs to help deal with unemployment, and self-exploration skills to help people create a sense of purpose.

The most productive approach is to determine the nature of the demands that are associated with stress, then analyze the person's skills for dealing with those demands. Where demands can be predicted, skill training can be undertaken in a proactive and preventive way. For example, teaching students the component skills in the Employability Skills Profile (McLaughlin, 1995) is a proactive step in helping to reduce stress associated with obtaining and maintaining employment. Similar programs could also be developed for dealing with other high frequency demands that were reported in earlier chapters of this book. The important point to emphasize here is that helping people deal more effectively with the demands they face (thereby reducing the likelihood of being overtaxed) is an important and legitimate way to control stress that often is overlooked in stress control programs. The role of schools and other educational institutions in skill training is obvious.

Some situations are so entrenched that they cannot be changed. In other cases the effort or amount of resources required to change a demanding situation may so extensive that it is not sensible to try to change the demand. It is also the case that some demands are so powerful that they overtax virtually everyone's coping ability. In such cases, stress may be unavoidable. In these types of cases, a person may not be able to avoid becoming stressed, BUT it still is possible to reduce the impact of the experience on the person. This is done by developing skills that help people stay calm when they are overtaxed and is referred to as **Stress Management. Stress Management** helps people change their reactions to situations by learning skills that help control the physiological, cognitive and behavioral components of the stress response.

Some form of regular relaxation is an effective way to help remain more calm in situations that are overtaxing. Ideally, some form of meditation, deep muscle relaxation or self-hypnosis is best, for they have well documented history of success for helping reduce stress. Hiebert (1993) outlines a detailed program for teaching deep relaxation that has demonstrated success in a wide variety of contexts with young adults, adolescents and younger school students (Hiebert, 1995). However, a less intense procedure called the Quieting Reflex, or QR for short, (Stroeble, 1983) also seems to work well for many people. A QR consists of taking 2, four-count breaths. You breathe in to the count of four and then out to the count of four. Then take a second four-count breath in and on the second four-count breath out, you let your jaw sag and imagine a wave of relaxation that flows down from your jaw to your chin, then up through your face, across the top of your head, down through your neck and shoulders, biceps, forearms, and wrists, hands and fingers, down through your body, and into your legs, ankles and feet, all the way down to the tips of your toes. When you catch yourself starting to tense up, you can take 20 seconds and do a QR to help you remain calm. On a busy day, you might stop every 20 to 30 minutes to do a QR just to make sure you don't end up getting too hyper. QR is not as effective as a full-blown relaxation training program, but many people see a noticeable difference when they use QR on a regular basis

Cognitive approaches to stress control focus on reducing people's tendency to exaggerate and put themselves down, while increasing a positive attitude. The comments made earlier in this chapter regarding building self-esteem are all appropriate for helping to control the cognitive component of the stress response. Using the "+/- card" or posting positive reminders are excellent ways to help maintain a more positive and encouraging mental attitude. People who have developed the ability to see the positive side of a situation experience less stress in those situations. Looking for the positives in a situation or providing self-encouragement should not be misinterpreted as a Pollyanna attitude. It simply refers to focusing on the parts of a situation that can be used productively to emphasize strengths or assist in active problem solving. As one step towards developing that positive attitude, many people find it useful to take a positive break. Stop every 2 hours or so and think about what you have done that was nice, and tell yourself *"Well, done. It feels good!"*

Behavioral approaches to stress control focus on helping people slow down and be less hyper. A common slogan says: "The hurrieder I go the behinder I get." Often the hyper behavior that is part of stress not only leaves people rushing around when there is no need to rush, but results in them making mistakes which in turn create additional demands. Another common saying is: "You may not have enough time to do it right, but you always have enough time to do it over." Simply slowing down the pace and working more systematically can reduce the harried feeling that accompanies stress and at the same time increase productivity. To be specific you may consider doing things like: walking slower, talking slower, taking a few minutes more to eat lunch (especially on busy days), completing tasks one at a time rather than trying to do everything at once, stopping for a short break mid-morning and mid-afternoon often helps to enhance a feeling of peacefulness and calm. Forcing oneself to slow down is especially important on days that are tightly scheduled. In a related vein, sometimes it is useful to simply leave a stressful situation briefly in order to regain ones composure and then try again to resolve the situation. Stress has sometimes been called the "Hurry-Up Syndrome." People can help combat the tendency towards hyper behavior that is part of the stress response simply by slowing down. Often simply slowing down will help people get more done and get it done with less stress.

Skills for dealing with academic demands

Academic demands are a frequently reported stressor by students of all ages. Dealing successfully with academic demands involves a broad skill set that incorporates several elements. The first step is address the obvious: is the student attending classes, focusing on the content of the classes and not daydreaming; does the student have good note-taking skills, a suitable space to study; has the student in fact been studying the material, and so on? Although it seems obvious, many people do not make the connection between these factors and academic success (Hunter, 1985).

The next step is to check out skill areas that are involved in academic success. This includes skills such as: note taking, time management, exam writing and study skills. It is important to take class notes that contain the important material and to organize them logically. If there is any doubt, students might check their notes against those of other class members, or approach their course instructors to confirm whether the important material has been copied down. Time management skills are also important for helping people complete their work more quickly and with more satisfaction. Most time management strategies include many simple things such as: preparing a study schedule, scheduling the fun activities after the work has been completed, scheduling 5-10 minute breaks every 60-90 minutes, incrementing large tasks into several smaller tasks, making a "To Do" list, posting it in a prominent place in the work area and crossing off each item as it is completed.

Systematic study skills are also important. It is one thing to spend large amounts of time studying, but that doesn't guarantee that the time has been spent profitably. One excellent study procedure is SQ3R. The acronym stands for Survey, Question, Read, Recite, Recall (see Rice, 1992; Grassick, 1992). First the student SURVEYS the material to obtain an overview of what the material is all about, and to prepare important QUESTIONS that should be able to be answered after the material has been studied. These QUESTIONS are written down for future reference. Then the student READS the material in a focused way to find out the answer to the questions. Each time the answer to a question is reached, the student pauses to RECITE the answer to the question several times. Finally, after the reading is completed, the student looks at the list of questions and tries to RECALL the answer to each question. For any question that cannot be answered during the RECALL stage, the person cycles back through the 3Rs, READING the answer again, RECITING it several times, then trying to RECALL the answers to all the questions again. Students who follow this pattern find that it takes them longer to go through the material initially, but, in the long run it saves them time because they recall more from the first time through.

Exam writing skills also are important. Most good students have a strategy for writing exams. Usually the strategy is a variation on the following. First, skim-read through the entire exam to get an idea of the questions and what is required. Then work through the exam, doing only those questions that you are sure you can answer correctly. Next, work through the exam again, answering those question that you know something about, but where you are not positive about your answer. If the exam is multiple choice, it may be possible to rule out some of the choices and find the correct answer through a process of elimination, or reduce the number of sensible alternatives from four or five to two or three. Finally, go through the exam a last time guessing at the answers to all the remaining questions. If the exam is multiple choice, and there is no penalty for guessing, then you have one chance in four of guessing correctly if the question has four possible answers. If you have eliminated one or two of the alternatives previously, then you can improve your odds at guessing correctly.

One final word on writing exams is in order. Often when people acquire skills for mastering the material on the test, and develop a strategy for getting that knowledge onto the test paper, they are less anxious about writing exams (Hunter, 1985). However, others find that they are anxious writing exams even though they are well-prepared. For these people it often is beneficial to use a combination of the stress control procedures outlined earlier when they are in the exam situation. This might involve using the Quieting Reflex to help control jittery muscles, nervous stomachs, sweaty palms or more serious symptoms like headaches. People who experience interfering self-talk (e.g., "You're going to goof this up again," or "I can't write exams," or "I always get nervous and forget everything I've studied") often benefit from a cognitive approach aimed at developing more positive and encouraging self-talk patterns, (e.g., "You studied lots and can remember the information, you'll do OK!"). Several studies of such procedures have consistently demonstrated success (e.g., Haynes et al., 1983).

Skills for developing an active, healthy lifestyle

Most estimates suggest that about 80% of all medical problems are due to lifestyle factors (Albrecht, 1979). The Heart and Stroke Foundation reports that in Canada there are over 18 million physician visits every year are due to cardiovascular problems in which lifestyle factors play a major role. Furthermore, stress and other lifestyle factors are thought to play a major role in other diseases such as: colds, flu, diabetes, cancer, multiple sclerosis and depression. Compounding such problems are the common maladaptive ways in which people react to stress which include: smoking, excessive use of alcohol, over-or-under-eating, increased use of stimulants such as coffee, tea and cola drinks, and use of over-the-counter drugs and street drugs. On the other hand, programs designed to promote a more healthy lifestyle have demonstrated success in reducing stress, increasing fitness, improving nutrition, increasing worker satisfaction and productivity, and improving general life satisfaction (Baydala et al., 1998; Malec & Hiebert, 1997).

Programs aimed at helping people attain a more balanced lifestyle (e.g., Malec et al., 1997) usually focus on several areas such as: nutrition, physical exercise, stress control and habit change. Nutrition education usually includes suggestions for reducing caffeine intake, reducing refined sugar, increasing Vitamin B, moderating alcohol consumption and maintaining a balanced diet. Regular exercise is emphasized. The type of exercise seems to be less important than the regularity and frequency with which it is practiced. Recent findings (e.g., Baydala et al., 1998; Malec & Hiebert, 1997) suggest that it is not necessary to be an "exercise devotee" in order to see positive results. Regular, moderate exercise is sufficient to yield significant gains in fitness, reductions in stress, increased general personal satisfaction. The stress control portion of lifestyle programs usually contain some combination of the suggestions for stress control contained in this chapter. Most effecting lifestyle change programs have a strong habit management overlay, similar in content to the general suggestions presented at the outset of this chapter (Prochaska et al., 1994). Thus, the information presented in this chapter can be helpful in preparing youth to meet the life transitions they will face, but as well, they can be useful in helping all people attain a more balanced lifestyle.

The Role of Adults in Youth Transitions

For the most part, adults can take an active role in helping to prepare youth to deal successfully with the life transitions they will encounter. Initially, this can be done by making sure the demands placed on young people are reasonable and that young people have adequate skill sets with which to meet the demands they face. Elkind (1981) points out that many parents keep their children excessively busy. This regimen is coupled with pressure on the part of some parents and teachers to have children grow up as quickly as possible. Children sometimes "graduate" from nursery school in caps and gowns. Elkind refers to this as the "miniature adult syndrome" and points out that children subjected to too many adult experiences too soon often find themselves in situations where the expectations placed on them are more than they can handle. As an alternative, he suggests that adults have a responsibility to make sure that the demands they place on children and youth are reasonable and appropriate, given the age and skill repertoires of the young people.

In school settings, teachers can help reduce demands through practices such as the following: setting specific and explicit grading criteria and sharing those grading criteria with students; establishing reasonable classroom routines so that classrooms become more predictable; presenting well-organized lessons where the logical connections between concepts is made explicit to students; reducing interruptions in instructional presentations; using co-operative (instead of competitive) games; being flexible to respond to individual learner characteristics; helping children set realistic goals regarding their achievement; increasing the amount of positive feedback students receive so as to enhance academic self-concept; and helping students develop inner control (i.e., a sense of personal agency or internal locus of control) (D'Aurora & Fimian, 1988; Dougherty & Deck, 1984). In addition, school programs aimed at addressing the whole person needs of youth, rather than focusing strictly on academic subjects, will help to reduce stress and better prepare young people for the transitions they will face (see Diachuk et al., 1995; Gysbers, 1990; Hiebert et al., in press; Millar, in press).

In summarizing research in this area, Yamamoto, Soliman, Parsons and Davies (1987) conclude that stress as experienced by young people, and adult estimates of the stress the young people experience, frequently are very different. Canadian research also suggests that the perceptions of adults and young people often differ markedly (Collins & Angen, 1997; Collins & Hiebert, 1995; Hiebert, Collins & Cairns, 1994). One important implication from such findings is that **a young person's perception** of the situation is the crucial factor in determining the adequacy of preparation for dealing with the demands that are being encountered. This means that adults should be cautious about placing youth in situations that they (youth) do not feel adequately prepared to handle. It is important also to make sure that the educational and family experiences that young people experience provide them with the skills required to successfully navigate the broad range of transitions they will encounter.

Conclusion

It has often been said that children are our most precious natural resource. It is important that we are wise and prudent stewards of this resource. Parents, educators, community leaders and policy makers need to be guided by a vision that values youth for who they are, not for their business, taxes or revenue potential. It is important for society to provide a supportive environment that creates a sense of belonging for all youth. It is necessary to create a milieu that helps young people have meaning and purpose in life, a sense of identity and pride in themselves and their communities, personal aspirations and a belief in self that fosters success. We need to strengthen and reinforce individual and community resources, while minimizing the threats, barriers and impeding forces. It is important also to provide training, counselling and other experiences that will foster the development of a broad enough skill set that enables young people to implement a personal vision for living.

It is important to realize that there are naturally occurring cycles that people go through when making changes in their lives. There is much contemplation, and often a certain amount of angst, before a person is ready to take action. When a decision is made to take action, there are definite strategies that people can follow that will help them feel empowered and become active agents in the change process. For the most part, having a broad repertoire of personal skills and other resources for dealing with the demands involved in the transition process, will help to smooth the transition process and promote success. It is important for adults to provide the learning experiences that will help equip young people for success. It is important for young people to avail themselves of the opportunities that will help to prepare them to face transitions with confidence and a sense of purpose.

Transitions are complex processes that are non-linear and last a lifetime. They are mediated experiences, therefore, amenable to influence. Individual and social factors contribute positively and negatively in optimizing transition experiences. An adequate repertoire of skills, and other coping resources, is important for maximizing the chances of dealing with transitions successfully. This can only be done if society recognizes the new and changing context youth are experiencing and develops comprehensive approaches to meet individual and group needs. The pay off for spending the time and resources required to adequately prepare youth to meet the demands they face is an increased chance of helping youth make successful transitions to fulfilling and productive lives. This definitely is worth the investment.

References

Albrecht, K. (1979). *Stress and the manager: Making it work for you.* Englewood Cliffs: Prentice-Hall.

Allen, S. & Hiebert, B. (1991). Stress and coping in adolescents. *Canadian Journal of Counseling, 25,* 19-32.

Amundson, N. E., Borgen, W. A. & Tench, E. (1995). Counselling and the role of personality and intelligence. In D. K. Saklofske & M. Zeidner (Eds.). *International handbook of personality and intelligence*. New York: Plenum.

Arthur, N. & Hiebert, B. (1996). Coping with the transition to post-secondary education. *Canadian Journal of Counselling, 30*, 93-103.

Bandura, A. (1995). *Self-efficacy in changing societies*. Cambridge, MS: Cambridge University Press.

Bandura, A. (1997). *Self-efficacy: The exercise of control*. New York: W. H. Freeman.

Baydala, A., Malec, C. & Hiebert, B. (1997). Lifestyle interventions, stress, and fitness. Paper presented to the annual meeting of the Canadian Psychological Association, Edmonton, Alberta.

Billings, A. G. & Moos, R. H. (1981). The role of coping resources and social resources in attenuating the stress of life events. *Journal of Behavioral Medicine, 4*, 139-157.

Borgen, W. A. & Amundson, N. E. (1995). Models of adolescent transition. In B. Hiebert (Ed.), *Exemplary career development programs and practices: The best from Canada*. Greensboro, NC: ERIC/CASS Clearinghouse

Collins, S. & Hiebert, B. (1995). Coping with the future: Challenging traditional beliefs about what adolescents need. In M. Van Norman (Ed.). *Natcon 21* (pp. 91-99). Toronto, ON: University of Toronto Career Centre.

Collins, S. &, Angen, M. (1997). Adolescents voice their needs: Implications for health promotion on suicide prevention. *Canadian Journal of Counselling, 31*, 53-66.

Compas, B. E. (1987). Coping with stress during childhood and adolescence. *Psychological Bulletin, 101*, 393-403.

Compas, B. E., Malcarne, V. L. & Fondacaro, K. M. (1988). Coping with stressful events in older children and young adolescents. *Journal of Consulting and Clinical Psychology, 56*, 405-411.

D'Aurora, D. L. & Fimian, M. J. (1988). Dimensions of life and school stress experienced by young people. *Psychology in the Schools, 25*, 44-53.

Davey Baustad, T. J. (In press). Junior high school interventions for student stress and workload. *Guidance and Counselling*.

Diachuk, C., Edwards, M., Gillis, S., Kirkland, G., Starko, T., Tomko, T. & Whelan, C. (1995). *From position to program: Building a comprehensive guidance and counselling program*. Edmonton, AB: Alberta Education.

Dougherty, A. M. & Deck, M. D. (1984). Helping teachers to help children cope with stress. *Journal of Humanistic Education And Development, 23*, 36-44.

Elkind, D. (1981). *The hurried child*. Reading, MA: Addison-Wesley.

Greenberg, J. S. (1990). *Managing stress: A personal guide*. Dubuque: Wm. C. Brown.

Gysbers, N.C. (1990). A model comprehensive guidance program. *Comprehensive guidance programs that work*. Ann Arbor, Michigan: ERIC CAPS.

Haynes, C. R., Marx, R. W., Martin, J., Wallace, L., Merrick, R. & Einarson, T. (1983). Rational-emotive counselling and self-instruction training for test anxious high school students. *Canadian Counsellor, 18*, 31-38.

Hiebert, B. (1988). Controlling stress: A conceptual update. *Canadian Journal of Counselling, 22*, 226-241.

Hiebert, B. (1991). Nature and treatment of stress-related problems in schools. In R. Short, L. Stewin & S. McCann (Eds.). *Educational psychology in Canada* (pp. 210-232). Toronto ON: Macmillan.

Hiebert, B. (1993). *Learn to relax: A self-help manual*. Toronto, ON: Lugus Productions.

Hiebert, B. (1995). Relaxation in the Classroom: A Program for Students and Teachers. Paper presented to the Annual Meeting of the American Educational Research Association, San Francisco.

Hiebert, B. & Eby, W. (1985). The effects of relaxation training for grade 12 students. *The School Counselor, 32*, 205-210.

Hiebert, B. & Malcolm, D. (1988). Cognitive strategies for mentally handicapped clients. In B. O'Byrne, (Ed.). *Natcon-14* (pp. 289-298). Toronto, On: Ontario College Counsellor's Association.

Hiebert, B., Collins, S. & Cairns, K. V. (1994). What do adolescents need?: Adult versus student perceptions. In M. Van Norman (Ed.), *Natcon-20: National Consultation on Vocational Counselling Papers*. (199-207). Toronto, ON: University of Toronto Career Centre.

Hiebert, B., Kemeny, K. & Kurchak, W. (In press). Guidance-related needs of junior high school students. *Guidance and Counselling*.

Hiebert, B., Kirby, B. & Jeknavorian, A. (1998). School-based relaxation: Attempting primary prevention. *Canadian Journal of Counselling, 23*, 273-287.

House, J. S. (1981). *Work stress and social support*. Reading, MA: Addison-Wesley.

Hunter, W. J. (1985). Getting wise to test anxiety. *The School Guidance Worker, 40*(4), 12-16.

Hutchinson, N. (1995). Career counselling of youth with learning disabilities. In B. Hiebert (Ed.), *Exemplary career development programs and practices: The best from Canada*. Greensboro, NC: ERIC/CASS Clearinghouse.

Kanfer, F. H. & Gaelick-Buys, L. (1991). Self-management methods. In F. H. Kanfer & A. P. Goldstein (Eds.), *Helping people change: A textbook of methods* (4th ed.)(pp. 305-360). New York: Pergamon.

Lazarus, R. S. & Folkman, S. (1984). *Stress, appraisal, and coping*. New York: Springer.

Lessard, J. J. (In press). Adolescent stress and workload: From bamboo seed to flying. *Guidance and Counselling*.

Mahoney, M. J. & Thoresen, C. E. (1974). *Self-control: Power to the person*. Monterey, CA: Brooks/Cole.

Mailandt, W. (In press). Adolescent perception of workload and stress. *Guidance and Counselling*.

Malec, C. & Hiebert, B. (1997). Exercise and stress: Two benefits for the price of one. *WellSpring, 8*(2), 7.

Malec, C., Young, L., Hiebert, B., Felesky-Hunt, S. & Blackshaw, K. (1997). *Stress medicine: You matter too (An intervention guide for building a healthy lifestyle)*. Calgary, AB: LifeLong Wellness Research Institute.

Martin, J. & Martin, W. (1983). *Personal development: Self-instruction for personal agency*. Calgary: Detselig Enterprises Ltd.

Mason, L. J. (1980). *Guide to stress reduction*. Culver City, CA: Peace Press.

McLaughlin, M. A. (1995). Employability skills: What are employers looking for? In B. Hiebert (Ed.), *Exemplary career development programs and practices: The best from Canada*. Greensboro, NC: ERIC/CASS Clearinghouse

Meichenbaum, D. (1985). *Stress inoculation training*. New York: Pergamon.

Millar, G. (In press). Guidance and Counselling in Alberta: Moving Toward Accountability. *Guidance and Counselling*.

Noer, D. M. (1993). *Healing the wounds*. San Francisco, CA: Jossey-Bass.

Posterski, D. & Bibby, R. (1988). *Canada's youths: "Ready for today": A comprehensive survey of 15-24 year olds*. Ottawa, ON: The Canadian Youth Foundation.

Prochaska, J. O., Norcross, J. C. & Diclemente, C. (1994). *Changing for good*. New York; Avon.

Reeh, E., Hiebert, B. & Cairns, K. (1998). Adolescent health: The relationships between health locus of control, beliefs, and behaviors. *Guidance and Counselling, 13*(3), 23-29

Rice, P. L. (1992). *Stress and health* (2nd ed.). Monterey, CA: Brooks/Cole.

Schlichter, K. (1978). An application of stress inoculation training in the development of anger-management skills in institutionalized juvenile delinquents. *Dissertation Abstracts International, 38*, 6172(b).

Stroebel, C. F. (1983). *QR: Quieting Reflex training for adults*. New York: Bantam.

Tocher, M. (1998). *Brave work: A guide to the quest or meaning in work*. Ottawa, ON: Canadian Career Development Foundation.

Yamamoto, K., Soliman, A., Parsons, J. & Davies, O. L. Jr. (1987). Voices in unison: Stressful events in the lives of children in six countries. *Journal of Child Psychology and Psychiatry an Allied Disciplines, 28*, 855-864.

Chapter 4
Matches and Mismatches in Student and Employer Perceptions

E. Lisbeth Donaldson

Introduction

The way we think about situations influences decisions because our perceptions are lenses that shape understandings. Students and employers are both involved in the transition from school to work process, but they may have differing perceptions about what contributes to success. As they make decisions about employability, both contend with social megatrends such as demographics, work place profiles, supply and demand dynamics, economics and requisite skill sets.

Mid-century technologies and postwar wealth contributed to the development of a social class called "teenagers" and a social movement called "feminism." Thus, change has replaced progress, accelerating to the point where demographers delineate generational differences. Those categorized as part of the Baby Boomer, Generation X and Baby Bust, and Echo Boomer decades live quite differently from their grandparents and parents. The match between education and employment also differs. Front-end Boomers have been successful, but as Foot (1996) explains, those who arrive late for general seating events do not get the best ones. Therefore Generation X, the late arrivals of the Boomer cycle, have fewer career opportunities than those in the early part of the cycle or the smaller, younger group that follows. This supply and demand dynamic has little to do with the quality or type of education or marketplace growth and recession cycles, but it is an interface that has obscured transition issues. Educators and employers very slowly are learning to stop blaming each other and to focus upon the problem: the development and induction of new talent that ensures cultural continuity and vitality. While it is unlikely, and perhaps undesirable, that their perspectives are identical with respect to how 15-30 year old citizens move from student to adult status, they do share a common interest in the youths' success.

The transition process will never be easy, but it also has been more difficult during the latter decades of the century because of the changed nature of the work place. Even the low-level student labor market has been computerized, but high-level face-to-face skills are required in service franchises that represent a global marketplace. The transient nature of student employment foreshadows new realities in the adult labor market. Employment cycles are more likely to be seasonal or project-length. Fewer employer benefits means more of an entrepreneurial attitude toward both government supported programs and personal long-term planning. Life on the information highway requires super-speed syntheses of knowledge, balanced with time for reflective "refills." Inequities in the labor force may increase, requiring intervention strategies that are focused, short-term in their implementation, but long-term in their effectiveness. Much more assessment and evaluation research needs to be conducted before matches between program and person and productivity are more generally satisfactory throughout youth cohorts.

It is improbable, however, that good matches between labor supply and demand will ever become a tight fit. A core democratic value is the freedom of choice and acceptance of the consequences. Nevertheless, many individuals think they make personal choices when, in fact, they are influenced by massive social forces such as technological development, government debt, civic disruption in other countries, ecological disturbances and infectious disease. Thus, a good fit might be a 5% unemployment level: a lower percentage means scarcity of labor in key areas and a higher one results in public deficits for support programs. A 25-year career in the same company is no longer the career profile of most adults, but 25 years in the labor force, properly planned within the total life span with phase-in and phase-out cusps, could be the employment profile of most adults. Women who mother might interrupt or plateau career aspirations, stretching the profile an extra decade; however, most of the basic desires of an adult, including education, home, financial security, and enjoyable hobbies could be earned with a 25-year financial plan.

The economics of education and employment has higher priority 50 years after the post-war boom. In a 1992 address to the Business and Education Conference of the Board, Judith Maxwell, Chair of the Economic Council of Canada, noted that Canada spent 22% of the GNP per capita on public education, arguing for a Canadian model that included choice, a core curriculum, diagnostic testing and remedial attention, a balance of vocational and academic priorities, integration of schooling and work experience and clear signals from employers so that the country maintains its global position. Consequences of high levels of participation in education are a quality of life: enriched appreciation of the fine arts, cultural diversity, sporting activities and relatively low levels of societal violence. But current retrenchment policies have had an impact. Reluctance to increase public debt impacts educational delivery, forcing reorganization; increased speed of competition contributes to downsized corporations, personal debts rise because of tuition and textbook expenses and fewer comprehensive benefits for employees are available. Reassessment of personal and public financial obligations requires a review of basic values. Education is important to society, so is employment to an individual. Therefore, mismatches between students and employers need to be monitored for wastage. Matches between students and employers must be strengthened if vitality and creativity are to be cultivated and harvested for the good of all.

Poor communication between adult advisors of youth in transition results in disjointed and sometimes conflicting suggestions that do little to hold fragmented lifestyles together. Since there is little agreement about when a young person becomes an adult, the transition from school to work is complicated by personal as well as professional milestones. Legal markers are not consonant: rights to vote and to work, licenses to drive, drink or marry are granted in different years of life. Family and peers profoundly impact the transition process as full-time student becomes full-time employee; educators become background mentors while employers move into the central role. Thus the various constellations of skill sets presented later in this discussion are developed by adult mentors who may not know each other and who may have differing opinions. Nevertheless, they indicate that difficulties navigating the passage may be reduced for many youth. One almost unrecognized aspect of the transition process is the personal maturity that evolves from trying to make sense of these complexities.

Perceptions often are accurate about context but hazy on details. This chapter is a discussion about employer and student perceptions of matches and mismatches in transitions between education and employment. Reference is made to educators, family and friends and peers who also influence the transition. Important trends are identified; some problems and solutions are outlined. But the major conclusion is that while progress has been made with respect to understanding the complexities of the transition process, much more work needs to be done by all involved if young people are to maximize their talents in ways that enrich their lives and invigorate society.

Employer Perceptions and Mismatches

Undoubtedly the key player for the employers is the Toronto-based Conference Board of Canada, the most important lobbyist group in the country. Gradually the Board has moved from a position that was a rather naive critique of educational systems to honoring educational innovators at high profile annual events and to producing useful resource materials. Other Foundations and employer organizations have also contributed substantially. At the post-secondary level, the Corporate-Higher Education Forum conducts research about transition issues. However, large corporations (with shrinking numbers of employees) are more likely to be members of these non-government organizations than are growth-oriented small and medium-sized employers; thus, employer involvement with youth programs may have more of a service orientation than an employment prospectus.

Established in 1954, the Conference Board of Canada has 700 Associate organizations with the mission of being "the leading private applied research institution dedicated to enhancing the performance of Canadian organizations within the global economy" (*at a glance* pamphlet, undated). It has 12 programs, of which the National Business and Education Centre addresses the "impact of changes in education on competitiveness" and "strategies for business involvement in public education." Although it claims to be "non-policy prescriptive," it has influenced national program development and demise as well as local school business-education partnerships (1996). Part of the success is the sustained commitment to change and the increasing quality of its publications. Like many other stakeholders involved in education-employment linkages, little follow-up research has been done with respect to the effectiveness of Board initiatives but the impact upon education policymakers is unquestioned.

The Employability Skills Profile published by the Conference Board of Canada in the early 1990s has been an exceptionally widely circulated pamphlet. Millions have been distributed nationally and internationally to employers, educators, community agencies and government officials. The Profile is a list of 26 "critical skills required of the Canadian Workforce." These include academic skills (such as communication, thinking and lifelong learning), personal management skills (such as positive attitudes and behaviors, responsibility and adaptability) and teamwork skills (including the ability to work with others in an organizational environment). The Board now notes that individual and school development of these "foundational skills" is "one of several goals, all of which are important for society" (1996, p. 108).

Closing the Gap, Women's Advancement in Corporate and Professional Canada (1997) is a 25-page booklet that tracks gains and barriers faced by women executives, most of whom earn more than $100 000 per year. The survey, done in conjunction with Catalyst, an American organization, concludes that work place perceptions that women can't manage challenging work and family ties contribute to their hesitation to utilize flexible work options offered by employers. Also, the women identified "inhospitable work environments and attitudes" as barriers to advancement while chief executives named a lack of relevant experience and "inadequate time in the leadership pipeline" (Conference Board of Canada/Catalyst, 1997, pp. 20-21). These differing perceptions are based in fact: although the participation of women has increased to 50% of the labor force, the talent pool remains heavily concentrated in 3 of 12 occupational groups: clerical, professional and service occupations (O'Neill, 1991, p. 11).

One winner of the Conference Board of Canada National Partners in Education Awards is the Calgary Educational Partnership Foundation (CEPF). Executive Director Doug Clovechok, a former teacher, positioned the Foundation to facilitate better business-education partnerships amongst the 200 members, including six school districts. CEPF (1996) produced the Employability Skills Portfolio Workbook for junior high school students and their teachers, but many parents have adapted the "creating my future" portfolio guidelines for their own disrupted careers. Many local key employers, members of the Foundation, now ask youth they interview for summer and part-time employment to bring a portfolio with them. However, within school environments, teachers and students demonstrated a considerable range of responses when using the portfolio. A rare example of a follow-up evaluation of transition issue initiatives indicated that when "there was a school-wide focus on career development, there was more extensive coverage of the employability skills and a higher rate of use of the teacher guides" (Hiebert & Tanner, 1995, p. 10). Otherwise both students and teachers tended to extract items from the portfolio without much sense of the transition process into which the graduating students were entering. Much more research needs to be done by all involved with respect to how resource materials are used and what programs are most effective.

As a reflection of employer interest in student retention and achievement, specialized programs have developed for targeted groups at both ends of the scales. Educational Partnership Foundation program activities include the Nakiska Ski day, an introduction of business executives to students who are at risk of early withdrawal or underachievement; the teachers-in-business project places educators during the summer in "curriculum-related businesses or organizations for a four to six week paid work and professional experience" (1997, 2). Another winner of the Conference Board of Canada Board Community Participation Award Program is the Shad Valley Summer Program for gifted high school science students who are placed in technological and science work place sites in an effort to "hothouse" their talent and interest. These CEPF and Shad Valley projects address youth who are not targeted by government programs such as the Boys and Girls Club *Vamos a Trabajar* (Let's Get Working) and other Youth Employment Committee organizations that support disadvantaged young people (Bowhay, 1994). However, a lack of coordination and poor communication creates interface gaps between these service organizations and the business sector: some students have access to many support services while average students may have none (Donaldson, 1995).

An example of corporate involvement, Petro-Canada is a leader in the School Resources Program of the Educational Partnerships Foundation. "It offers several welcomed advantages to our company: a single contact, simplified logistics, an opportunity to participate in a true community effort, and the assurance that our surplus items will be distributed according to need" (CEPF, 1997). Usable surplus resources donated to schools during a period of "fiscal pressures" included computers, binders, and furniture. "Binders are a big cost item for small schools; your donation enables us to use budget funds in other ways that will benefit our students," commented one principal of an elementary school. Petro-Canada also has a scholarship program for its part-time student employees. The amounts students receive are only a few hundred dollars, but they are a significant acknowledgement of the youth's efforts. Many winners hope to establish an employment cycle that moves them from a high school gas jockey to a corporate accountant, human resource consultant or an engineer within the corporation. It's an unanticipated benefit for the corporation that is then well positioned to select from a larger pool of educated youth, already knowledgeable about its corporate culture.

Making the Match, a five-stage follow-up of university students from the time they were undergraduates to mid-career cycles, was a study commissioned by the Corporate-Higher Education Forum (Evers, Rush, Krmpotic, Duncan-Robinson, 1993). Restricted to major corporations, it nevertheless identified variations in core competencies during these stages and differences between student/employee and employers. A more recent study encourages youth to complete post-secondary education while urging educators to form more business partnerships (1997). Of the 75 Board, Honorary and Associate Members of the Corporate-Higher Education, 6 are women, a reflection of the gap reported by the Conference Board of Canada. Although this type of research is scarce, it suggests that the dynamics of the transition process are similar, regardless of when students depart educational systems. The major difference is that students who drop out from high school operate within an immediate local environment while those with graduate degrees have global opportunities and their search may take longer. Nevertheless, anxiety during the interim period reduces tendencies to explore options and mobilize resources unless the youth has prepared for the transition process.

Student Perceptions and Mismatches

Concern about youth employment escalated during the 1980s recession when double-digit youth unemployment rates became a national embarrassment: such squandering of young talent would eventually result in stasis, even in a wealthy, new country. Nevertheless, evidence of transition problems was apparent several decades earlier, masked by post-war economic momentum. Twenty years after the issue was recognized as a major societal issue, much is known about how to effectively reduce some problems, but there is still too much wastage of human and financial resources, still too many gaps and still too much distrust amongst adult advisors.

Young people in their 20s speak of "my school career," and why not! Urged by parents, teachers, employers and prompted by their own ambitions, many have spent the first quarter of their lives in educational institutions. They are school weary and school smart, but the only contact most have had with the work place is low level part-time employment: the "employed student" labor market, as this sector is now defined by government. Regardless of level of credentials achieved, students need to be educated in how to make the transition between education and employment; some university students are more at risk of being underemployed than are high school dropouts.

Initially the concern was one of rising social service costs that contributed to governmental debts. The argument was that high school dropouts were likely to withdraw more from multiple services, including welfare, health and community support groups, than they would ever contribute to society, and the resultant cumulative costs were so high they burdened middle class contributors. As marketplace dynamics became more unstable, unemployment patterns permeated all levels of society, affecting not only new high school graduates but many family wage earners. Thus, work, school, recreational and family activities juggled in highly individuated schedules gradually became "normal" for many fathers, mothers and their two children. These fragmented lifestyles have changed enrollment patterns in post-secondary institutions, although the "stay in school" initiative remains a foundational slogan.

Students between the ages of 15 and 25 (categorized as youth as work hours increase and educational contacts reduce) lead a fragmented lifestyle during which they gradually take more responsibility for decisions that have long term impact. Their circle of "consultants" shifts from family and teachers to friends and part-time employers. Regrettably, so much of the process is casual, often a cumulation of seemingly small events. A student earns a high grade in one class but not in another and decides not to pursue a subject area, or a friend dislikes a teacher, or a course is scheduled inconveniently early. A supervisor calls, needing a shiftwork replacement, and a class is skipped. A slightly reduced grade point average (GPA) seems a worthwhile tradeoff for a work experience resume citation, but the GPA is too low to obtain a scholarship or enter a desired professional school. As tuition and textbooks costs rise, so do the numbers of students who work, but the pattern was established in high school.

The part-time student labor market is a mixed opportunity. On the positive side, it helps students mature, simulating adult responsibilities. Students may learn useful employment skills such as interpersonal communication, applied math and technology, and time management. Canadian research data indicate that general level high school students often demonstrate improved academic achievement but achievers often suffer lower GPAs (Government of Canada, 1993). This dynamic is replicated in university, where students often work at low level employment to pay for tuition, to reduce stress or to have the illusion of adult status, but these "employed students" do not often realize that six years in the same part-time job may result in underemployment after graduation: over time the degree became the avocation. Students accustomed to a "school career" lifestyle, commuting between parental home, post-secondary education, and part-time work during their late teens and early 20s may be squandering opportunities to maximize their talents as adult citizens. By contrast, students who position themselves in career-related areas through 8 to 10 hours of weekly work or through volunteer activities enjoy accelerated career entry. They gain relevant experience, make contacts and understand what opportunities are available in related fields of work; sometimes the valuable lesson learned is that they do not want that type of career. The $2000 to $5000 income earned by most students during a school year becomes a monthly salary for a graduate who is appropriately employed.

Student loans have temporarily deferred interest rates, but even a $10 000 debt becomes an increasing burden when the time to completion of a post-secondary credential is extended for a year or two and a new loan is added. The average debt load for a 1994 university graduate in Alberta in 1994 was $15 293. The highest rates were amongst graduates where the "fit between current job and university program" was greatest, such as law and medicine, professions in which the loan could most quickly be paid off and in which an intensive time commitment is required before graduation (Krahn & Lowe, 1998). However, where the degree is less directly linked to a professional marketplace, although personal debt might be somewhat lower, postgraduate employment opportunities are less remunerative and time to completion of the degree may be prolonged because of fragmented lifestyles. Rarely does income from part-time employment over a period of four to five years (average $13 000 annually, higher amongst humanities students) equal that of full-time post graduation employment (average $37 000, lower amongst humanities degree holders). There is also gender differential in that more women graduate from the humanities; thus as students they work more part-time hours for less money and earn less upon graduation, taking a longer time to pay off education debts. Nevertheless, while women tend to earn lower incomes, the wage gap is smaller amongst university graduates than amongst those with less education.

Regardless of the mythology about unemployed university students, labor market statistics clearly indicate the value of educational credentials. The 18% of young people who have not completed high school by age 20 are more likely to have periodic layoffs and lower incomes; high percentages of them have Aboriginal origins or English as a Second Language background (Government of Canada, 1993; Watt & Roessingh,1994). By age 25, the national percentage drops to 15%; provincial rates vary from Prince Edward Island (21%) to Alberta and Saskatchewan (tied at 11%), suggesting intervention programs have some effect particularly for young women (Government of Canada, 1996).

Youth unemployment percentages are higher than those of older workers, but those who are university graduates have less unemployment (5.1%) than other post-secondary diplomas (7.7%) or high school graduates (9.4%) (Corporate-Higher Education Forum, 1997, quoting AUCC, 1996). The Statistics Canada National Graduates Survey of 1990 indicated that males with less than high school averaged $29 634 annually, but male university graduates earned $55 976 (Corporate Higher Education Forum, 1998). Females earn less: $20 637 with less than high school and $42 584 if university graduated. These figures vary considerably by region, but the general trends do not change: obtaining an educational credential is related to higher income, and gender does make a difference in the rate of return upon the educational investment.

Matches Between Student and Employer Perceptions

Student and employer interests are best matched when educational credentials are relevant, work experience develops employability skills, and linkage programs are effective. Creativity is an elusive quality, much respected but difficult to nurture.

At job entry, both prospective employee and employer are agreed that educational credentials act as a screening mechanism. Students know they must obtain a relevant certificate or an appropriate degree before they apply for specific occupations. Employers assess company needs and advertise for a specific type of employee. Alignments depend upon supply and demand. In some industries immigration reduces marketplace shortages of skilled labor, but Canada still lags behind other countries in research and development spending. It remains an anomaly of our culture that Canada spends more on kindergarten to grade twelve education, and has policies that facilitate accessibility to post-secondary institutions, but does not meet its technological and trades needs nor supply support for employment in new cutting-edge research fields. Canada does export highly trained professionals such as engineers, medical personnel and researchers to other countries, especially the well-known brain drain going south of the American border. However, for mid-range status occupational employment competitions, where a surplus of applications is problematic, employers assess other aspects of the student's employment profile more carefully.

Previous work experience is valued, but only if the resumé indicates relevant skill development. Those students who have learned to extract useable employability skills such as oral communication or teamwork can maximize the benefits from low level service employment. Volunteer experience in an area is an asset because it is a passport into an occupational constellation. Women use this approach more effectively than many men because they often want service-related careers in professional areas located in short-staffed public sector fields. For example, acceptance into the Faculty of Education is facilitated if the applicant already has volunteered time with young people: it is proof that the prospective teacher does like working with children. At graduation, if some volunteer work has been done in schools, references from established teachers are invaluable additions to the job entry application package.

Linkage programs to the marketplace have been implemented in many urban school systems during the past 15 years. These types of programs often involve cooperative education, work experience, job shadowing and parental work place visitations. When well-matched, they are a fast track to a career; even a partial match introduces students to complex work place cultures, encouraging analysis of organizational dynamics. If the match is poor, students may extract generic skill development in much the same way as they would for part-time work. The reality of linkage programs, however, is that in high school coop programs are for students who don't plan to go to university while in university coop programs are for high achievers. Work experience, job shadowing and career days are but brief exposures to adult careers. Many students have never visited their parents' employment site, do not know their job titles, and have no idea what are their tasks; the higher the level of occupation, the less likely the youth is to be familiar with the parental environment. One science student reported that both parents had Ph.Ds and worked in the oil patch downtown, but he didn't know what they did or what he wanted to do after completing his undergraduate degree.

Therefore, part-time work remains the strongest and most extensive link to the work place for most students. In Canada, citizens age 14-65 are entitled to work, excepting in heavy industry. The tradition of Friday night and Saturday jobs has been shared by both rural and urban youth for generations. What is new, especially in the rapidly growing cities, are opportunities to work during the week and on Sundays, thus competing with school schedules. Some high school students actually take credit courses during the evenings or summers and are employed in weekday shift work during the school term. Students who work more than 15 hours per week are unlikely to do well in school, although many persist to graduation. They risk becoming underemployed if employers think the best match for their skills is in the area of part-time work. Furthermore, they are undereducated. "I was a mental dropout," said one high school graduate, now working full time in a warehouse (Donaldson, 1992).

Because of great concern about negative personal and societal effects of leaving school before graduation, more is known about the transitions of dropouts and the remedial programs that attempt to redress the issues; much less is understood about the transition of students with Baccalaureate or Masters degree, or of those who apprenticed in programs that became redundant. The proportion of the labor market labelled "voluntary part-time workers" by the Federal government increased continually from 1975 to more than 11% of all employment in 1993 and the fastest growing group was the 43% attending school. Dropout profiles include: higher percentages of male students who work more than 20 hours per week while in school; female students who did not work at all, many of whom are aboriginal teenage mothers (Government of Canada, 1993). Intervention programs target the general youth population and target specific disadvantaged groups but evaluations that track long-term success rates are scarce (Alberta Intergovernmental Task Force, 1994; Bowhay, 1994). Some high school students do not continue directly to post-secondary education (26% in Alberta) but spend several years drifting in combinations of part-time student and work (Alberta, Career Development and Employment, 1992). There is less guidance for these youth, and for those who enter university directly but who flounder as an undergraduate. "Although women made up 45% of the total work force in 1993, they constituted 71% of voluntary part-time workers" and most had a child under age 6 at home (Logan, 1994, pp. 19-22). Thus, gender differentials also permeate the part time workplace.

National surveys of university graduates indicate that two years later, most are employed, but the relevance of their education to their employment is closest in fields such as medicine, dentistry and law and least in the social sciences and humanities, including those who had persisted to MA or MSc levels of education. While these general programs prepare individuals for a wide range of rewarding careers, they are less likely to obtain entry-level employment that results in them doing so (Krahn & Lowe, 1998). Because of the diffuse range of possibilities for employment and the cultivated individuation of a university education, trying to determine matches between education and employment is very difficult. Not much research has been done but the tendency is to focus upon skill generation and utilization rather than credentials.

Employability is important, but a good match between individual talent and employment position is what generates growth. In spite of all that is known about effective education strategies and learning styles, creativity remains one of the most elusive qualities to nurture. Teachers attempt to facilitate talent when it is demonstrated, but they want compliance when academic credits are on the line. Employers claim to desire "the ability to identify and suggest new ideas to get the job done" (Conference Board of Canada, Employability skill #19, 1996, 108), but they also want company productivity. Sometimes rebels do very well, regardless of credentials, but more frequently they burn out and do not sustain career momentum. Creativity is somehow connected with visualization and spirituality, self identity and discipline. Artists, athletes, scientists and some employers often nurture this aspect of talent. In a rapidly changing society, it is a precious "commodity." When employers and employees are well matched, it doesn't matter what the job title, what the organizational mission, what the product: what stimulates is the excitement generated in realizing the goal. Youth in transition who creatively match their talents with employment possibilities mix security with risk, catalysts for a good future.

Mismatches Between Student and Employer Perceptions

At least four types of mismatches contribute to differences between student and employer perceptions: a lack of understanding about the transition process, varying constellations of required skills, the impact of gender roles and poor communication among adult advisors. Other mismatches may cloud the hiring environment, such as the ratio of applicants to availability of jobs and naiveté about rapidly changing education and employment situations, but four basic mismatches persist through time and differences in occupational strata, causing misalignments that result in talent underutilization.

"There is a serious mismatch between dreams and realities," claims the Corporate-Higher Education Forum (1997, p. 24). Of the 100 young people featured as 1997 *Macleans* leaders of tomorrow, only five are in the sciences at a theoretical level and the average age of apprentices in Alberta is 29 (p. 19). The Forum report argues for a "set of core competencies" such as "logical thinking, ethics, teamwork, personal skills, eagerness to learn, information management, innovation, and creativity" and acknowledges the futility of educator-employer blaming if students do not demonstrate such skills. Among the new sophistication with respect to reducing transition problems is evidence that both educators and employers have learned to respect the complexities of the information age: no one formula will work but some solutions do. The "trick" is to assist students to develop skills specific to their changing environments. They are mostly process level skills that can be acquired as content is learned but may need workshop development to be effective.

Mismatches During the Transition Process

The exit from formal education initiates a highly individualized period of decision-making, but patterns of behavior among student cohorts have been identified. Regardless of whether students depart high school or university, the types of behaviors and the percentages of students within each category are similar (Donaldson, 1992, 1996). Some categories are more porous than others, that is, with support (or without it) students move from one classification to another. As well, adult advisors influence some patterns more than others; thus the classifications are not necessarily deterministic predictors of adult success. However, few youths understand the transition process as they leave education for employment, although many certainly struggle with the passage. Adult advisors within education or employment establishments participate in either end of the process, but only family and friends observe most of the longitudinal effects upon an individual in transition.

The six patterns of behavior that emerge during the transition process include the following descriptions. (See Illustration 1 for a visual schemata.)

- Regardless of whether schooling is compulsory or not, some students just *pass through* the system, having minimal contact. Perhaps they have parents who frequently move or who do not value formal education. While they are a minority of about 10% among their cohort, they often include high percentages of minority groups such as Aboriginal students, immigrants with language problems and transients who move because of parental occupations.
- Other students have serious *ongoing personal and social problems*. These disabilities may include drug and alcohol addictions, sexual abuse, learning impairments and physical diseases. Again, these students

are a minority statistic of about 10%, but they often consume limited social resources such as counsellor time.
- A few students have *bottleneck* difficulties, problems with the system that may be a clash with authority figures, late registration or poor performance in prerequisite courses, or some other barrier that is structural in nature. Often, this situation is a one-time occurrence but it might have a long-term effect if it results in a rejection of education.
- Nearly one-third of the students *flounder*, drifting aimlessly, confused about goals and opportunities. Most people experience floundering periodically in their lives but if sustained, the behavior contributes toward a downward drift of aspirations and achievement. This category is too large and if targeted by adult advisors, probably would result in more effective interventions than any other. These students need to acquire the constellation of skills necessary to success in their

**Illustration 1:
Three Stage Transition Process:
Seven Emergent Patterns of Behavior**

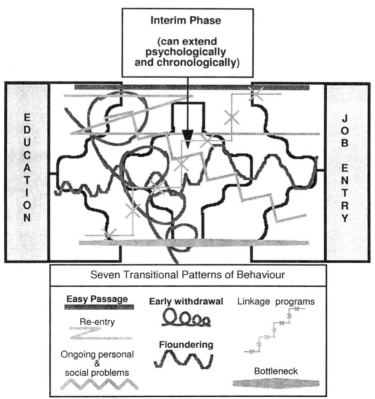

respective situations, but often educators, family and friends, and employers do not provide such support.
- Attracting mostly male students, *apprenticeship* programs link education to trade careers, but many who would do well in this area reject the status; in an society composed of immigrants, accessibility to university remains a desirable family achievement. Registered Apprenticeship Programs in high school give students an advantage in about 50 occupations as they earn money and credit toward a formal program; however, only about 6% of students leaving school select this option.
- Some students *re-enter* formal education after a period of two or more years. At all levels of education, this trend has increased steadily since mid-century, particularly marked by the presence of adult women. Sometimes motivated more by intrinsic reasons, these students have maturity, and are deeply interested in their studies. They often are ignored because their enrollment patterns tend to be hidden in spring, summer or evening enrollments.
- The largest category, hovering about the 50% level, is the one in which students report an *easy passage* between education and employment. It is a mark of success that so much diversity is addressed by educators and employers but the percentage could be increased if some problems in other categories were reduced. A decrease in the numbers of floundering students and increased percentages of apprenticeships would result in more students having an easy passage during the transition. This category could approximate 75% of the total cohort.

Skill Mismatches When Navigating Educational-Employment Transitions

To succeed in the goals of achieving educational credentials and obtaining career-level employment, several sets of skills are required. These constellations of skills overlap but priorities in each situation are not identical. The set of skills needed to achieve in educational systems is different from those that contribute to an easy passage between education and employment environments. Job entry skills differ from the employability skills necessary to career development. Few youth understand how to consciously develop and practice the necessary skill set; thus, learning is a combination of *ad hoc* opportunities and experimentation, not the best combination for an easy passage.

To succeed in educational goals, meta-curricular skills need to be explicitly articulated and honed. They include: time management, examination skills, communication skills (including written, oral and group dynamics), interpersonal, intrapersonal and critical thinking about content, an integration that results in synthesis.

However, different disciplines place varying emphases upon these skills and cutbacks affect delivery. Thus, some students receive little practice in writing while others might not have many oral assignments. Counselling services do provide workshops and some programs review courses with respect to how specific constellations of skill sets are developed, but there are gaps. Students who participate in first-year activities are more aware of how these skills contribute to undergraduate success. If more students realized how to use skills sets for academic achievement, their GPAs would undoubtedly rise as they acquired such expertise. The University of Calgary has defined five types of core competencies that all programs are to cultivate in students: critical and creative thinking, analysis of problems, effective oral and written communication, gathering and organizing information, logical calculation. However, a few years of post-secondary education are only an opportunity to practise: most of these competencies are lifelong acquisitions.

As students exit the educational system, a different set of skills is required. Transition skills, a slightly different constellation from employability skills, assist students when negotiating the passage between education and employment. One conceptualization of this transition period is a three-staged process: an in-school phase that ends when questions shift from "what are you taking in school?" to "what are you going to do when you leave school?"; an interim phase, both chronological and psychological; and a job entry phase that ends approximately 18 months after full-time employment has been obtained. (Illustration 1 indicates this process and the six patterns of emergent behavior.) The interim transition period often extends as the level of the educational credential increases, and sometimes a geographical move may be necessary. For example, a high school graduate often has fewer resources than a post-secondary graduate. Graduates with one degree or certification need an entrepreneurial attitude, regardless of specialization. Too frequently, they refuse career-level opportunities in the North or smaller cities, preferring underemployment near supportive parents and friends.

In addition to an educational credential, transition skills include job (re)search, contacts and networking, resume and reference, oral interview, and relevant part-time work or volunteer experience. The shift between a student level of employment (low level service jobs) to an adult labor market (career opportunities) is a large step for many youth. Anxiety about the future and uneven development of these skills makes the transition passage more difficult for some.

Job entry skills comprise a slightly different set of capabilities, some of which are taught in secondary school programs such as the Career and Technology Studies program approved by Alberta Education in September, 1997. Others are learned more informally, perhaps through work place exposure and experience. At the university level, Evers et al. (1993) identified "four base components of skill competence" among five career stages, including two undergraduate stages, job entry and job shifts. These four sets of competencies included: mobilizing innovation and change (creativity); managing people and tasks; communicating; managing self. Students tended to rate themselves higher than did employees in all categories; the realities of the labor force were sobering experiences. At job entry, new graduates rated themselves more highly on communicating and managing self, but in all career stages, the creativity component remained the lowest category of competency. Arts and social science graduates differed from engineering, ranking higher respective to communication and creativity skills. Females rated themselves higher in the relationships categories, males were higher on the creativity component, but differences were not statistically significant. However, managerial assessments of graduates rated new graduates lower and valued the creativity component more. Thus, perceptions about competencies vary during a career span and are more likely to differ between new graduates and employers at job entry.

Finally, employers generally support the Conference Board of Canada (1996) employability skills list which is organized into three subsets: academic, personal management and teamwork. Academic skills include communication, using the language of the business culture, listening, reading and writing; thinking critically and logically; problem-solving including mathematics, technology and other information tools, ability to apply and access specialized knowledge; and a commitment to lifelong learning. Personal management skills include positive attitudes and behaviors such as self-esteem and confidence, honesty and ethics, personal health and growth, energy and persistence; responsibility includes abilities to set personal and professional goals and priorities, management of time, money and other resources, accountability for actions; adaptability includes a positive attitude toward change, recognition and respect for diversity and individual differences, and creativity. Teamwork skills include an ability to work with others, contributing to the organization and culture of the group, planning and decision-making with support of the outcomes, respecting thoughts and opinions of others, the group dynamics of giving and taking, team and leadership roles as appropriate.

Summaries of the four sets of skills are in Table 1: meta-curricular, transition, job entry and employability. Overlap is obvious but the constellation of skill sets is specific to the various situations and priorities differ. Furthermore, these skill sets, as with all skills, need to be learned and polished. Few individuals are proficient in all of the subsets and/or only gradually develop a particular set of skills for the situation. The extent to which youth have not developed these constellations of skills contributes to mismatches in education-employment transitions.

Table 1:
Summary of skill constellations needed
to reduce mismatches in four situations

Meta-Curricular Aids to Education Achievement	Transition Skills that Facilitate the Process	Job Entry Core Competencies	Employability Skills for Career Development
time management	job (re)search	communication	academic
examination	contact/networking	managing self	personal management
communication	resume/reference	innovate/change	teamwork
interpersonal	oral/interviews	managing tasks	
content-integration	part-time work/volunteer experience		
intrapersonal			

Gender Role Mismatches

When achievements of the 20th century are listed, the changes in women's lives are likely to be among the more important that impacted society. During the early decades, legal gains included the vote, the right to own property and direct inheritance; mid-century gains included antibiotics and reliable birth control methods that ensured a full life span; late century achievements involved the exercise of public power in public and private sectors. Nonetheless, accessibility to further education did not immediately result in ascent up corporate ladders; women had to earn these positions and then ensure that other women were not excluded. As the

Conference Board of Canada (1997) indicates, an increase from 29 to 43% between 1982 and 1995 of managers and administrators is improvement, but it is not equity. Nevertheless, a critical mass has been reached and gendered participation in the marketplace is a megatrend that affects everyone.

Although the talent pool of female lawyers, medical doctors, scientists and executive officers has increased, differences in the female life cycle are still not considered normative. The woman's life cycle includes maiden, mid-life and crone phases; priorities include personal relationships (such as parents, children and spouses) as well as evidence that professional women select biological-oriented issues (such as family law, obstetrics and paediatrics, environmental research and sustainable ecological practices). Many women in the mid-life cycle are more successful establishing their own businesses than working within large organizational hierarchies. While a considerable body of feminist scholarship has contributed to an understanding about issues in women's lives, perceptions "that family commitments affect their work performance may make advancement to senior levels more difficult for some women" (Conference Board of Canada/Catalyst, 1997, p. 21). Women in the mid-life cycle are among the most stressed people in society and their problems are not well addressed.

Young women aged 15-30 are at the peak of their biological power and few know how to plan a life span that includes personal and professional achievement; many juggle the responsibilities, learning as they go through the paces. Women as role models, issues involving women (such as child care), ethics surrounding abortion are rarely on the curricula in social studies classes. The education of male spouses with respect to family issues is still mostly a high school sex education module or the frantic demands made by a harassed mother that some housework be done by her partner. It will take some time before employers during the hiring phase and women at job entry can talk honestly. At the moment employment equity issues are legislated, but implemented unevenly. Legislation is an early stage that establishes a foundation for societal change, but education is the long term mortar that melds public opinion.

Another mismatch between student and employer perceptions is naiveté about the two worlds of education and employment. Corporate personnel are more informed about educator values as a consequence of participation in programs such as those sponsored by the Calgary Educational Partnership Foundation, but they are still learning that each year a new cohort of school leavers faces the same set of challenges in a constantly changing work environment. The issues are perennial; the solutions are not. Furthermore, the most rapidly growing area of the business sector are companies with fewer than 50 employees, small to moderate organizations that have few resources for employee training and community involvement. These companies are less likely to be members of the Conference Board of Canada or the Corporate-Higher Education Forum. Thus, often students in linkage programs interact with representatives of organizations that are not expanding, but they "cream the crop" of new graduates when hiring. Most student contacts are limited to part-time work situations, unless they have family and friends in the growth work force areas. Therefore, many students still fall back upon informal networks when in transition. For example, one Ontario youth said he had always admired the neighbor who was a policeman, but when he graduated from high school, he realized that his Portuguese uncle, cousins, father and brothers were in construction and he decided to join them. A Calgary woman undergraduate leader realized in her last semester of a sociology degree that she had never job searched further than her part-time greenhouse employer a few blocks from the family home. Regardless of level of educational credential, although the point of entry into the marketplace might be different, many students, about to become employees, are afflicted with debilitative stage fright that narrows the range of options they seriously consider.

Mismatches Among Adult Advisors

Students becoming adults depend upon adult advisors to guide them through the passage, but most adults are too positioned within their respective roles to provide continuity. Furthermore, tensions between the various types of adult advisors result in poor communication that impedes the youth.

Often, there is a mismatch between student and employer regarding the role of education and of educators. For students, teachers often are the only adults with whom they have long term contact, excepting family and family friends and part-time employers. High school teachers are personal and professional mentors who may not know much about the marketplace, because they have never worked extensively outside of educational settings. Dialogue between teacher and student often concerns the high school to university transition, but many students who say they plan to attend post-secondary institutions do not follow through. Thus, it is possible for a well meaning teacher to offer poor advice about specific career paths. However, most teachers are well equipped to serve as references. Few are asked. Perhaps students fear personal weaknesses are too well-known; perhaps they don't think employers will value educator comments; perhaps there are other reasons. Whatever, in the one arena that teachers could best be used as a resource, they are rarely used unless they teach in a linkage program, such as cooperative education. At post-secondary institutions, students in career specific programs will ask instructors for references, but students in liberal arts and social science programs are expected to develop contacts independently.

Counsellor-youth mismatches with respect to early work experiences are also noted (Cairns, Woodward & Hashizume, 1992). Counsellor emphasis is upon employment skills, attitudes and expectations and employer characteristics; student emphasis is upon their lack of job search skills and their need for personal fulfillment as an adult developmental milestone. Even within the low level student labor market, many youth are jolted by marketplace experiences. Both counsellors and students agree that social support networks, whether linkage programs, family or agency-based skills programs, reduce negative consequences of the transition process.

On the other hand, most employers know what school is like; they also spent years there. However, they don't always know how the approaches to learning within the familiar and well-known building have changed. Thus, students educated from a student-centred perspective that encourages self-directed learning may be assessed as "motor-mouths" when observed by a corporate employer skilled in hierarchical power. Employers blaming "the educational system" could develop employee induction programs that hone general skills into specific ones, encouraging a creative integration and talent development. Critical thinking skills help integrate understandings of how systems differ in their dynamics, but few adult advisors assist students to evaluate their fragmented lifestyles. Teachers accepting assignments not completed on time or ignoring good grammar in lieu of originality may be developing attitudes in students whose work will devalued by those committed to sustaining a corporate image. The influence of part-time work upon youth in transition needs to be a curriculum item. As employer meets employee, rarely is the educator directly involved but the memory remains a powerful impact in both minds.

Parental and peer involvement in student transitions is an often ignored influence. During the interim phase of the transition process, their advice is often the most important, contributing substantially to the youth's decision-making (Crysdale, Donaldson & Joseph, 1987). These informal support systems provide continuity at a personal level while professional development is in a state of flux. If parental perspectives are not aligned with educators, students may be discouraged from further opportunities. If youth are uncertain about employment cultures that differ from family occupations, they may not search further than familiar role models. Sometimes parents offer too much support, unwittingly discouraging their fledglings from testing latent strengths in a more competitive world. Students who are reluctant to discuss their fears with parents may follow a friend's lead rather than developing personal goals. Part-time student labor market employers offer limited support, a false security that frequently leads to underemployment. Often the "drift" noted in government employment statistics among young people who are slow to establish careers during their 20s is a consequence of reliance upon informal personal networks and an uneven, slow development of the skill sets needed to make the transition from one educational or employment environment to another.

Finally, mismatches between disciplines of research, education and employers mirrors the general weakness regarding research and development in Canadian society. Sociologists Paul Anisef, Paul Axlerod (1996) and Paul Grayson (1994) at York University have reported differences between student intentions and actions. Harvey Krahn and Graham Lowe (1998) of the Human Population Laboratory in Edmonton, and Sid Gilbert (1993) and Fred Evers (1993) at the University of Guelph have been consulted by the Federal Government and the Corporate-Higher Education Forum to identify macro-level issues. Counselling psychologists such as Kathy Cairns (1992) probe micro-level problems among individual clients. Bryan Hiebert's evaluation of the Calgary Educational Partnerships Foundation Employability Portfolio (1995) is a rare example. But researchers situated within Faculties of Education, knowledgeable about program evaluation, curriculum development, student diversities and educational policies are rarely involved in such partnerships, although their work has a powerful impact upon teachers. Jane Gaskell's work (1992) on gender, widely used across Canada in teacher training courses, appears to be ignored by the business sector. Such research helps to identify complexities in the transition issue, but the time has come to move to program evaluation, to integrate learning styles with transition issues, to apply data regarding patterns of behavior to problems within the transition process, to focus upon interrelationships between skills and creativity. Business-education partnerships need not be short-term applications that band-aid wounds. If the rigor characteristically used for new research initiatives were applied, theory would inform practice in ways that effectively reduce transition problems and further insights would be gleaned from the application. Business-education partnership concepts must expand to include researchers in transition issues. Also, more multi-disciplinary research needs to be conducted between various academic disciplines.

The set of skills students need to survive educational systems is different from the skill set needed to make an easy passage through the transition process; the skill set needed to move from a student labor market to an adult labor market is yet another constellation, while skills needed within an occupation might be similar to those necessary to succeed in school, but they might not be if the organization dynamic is quite different. These four sets of skills overlap and in some cases may be mostly a reordering of priorities. But no research has been conducted that indicates how these skills sets may be learned, integrated and applied. Instead, lists of skills are developed and handed out to youth, who are usually terrified about their ability to develop such mastery and uncertain about where to go to ask for assistance. However, the emergent consensus during the 1990s about the importance of skill constellations is an important development. Undoubtedly, the next decade will result in more integration.

Conclusions

Megatrends establish the societal context within which annual cohorts of youth make the transition from education to full-time employment. Among these thousands of young people, various patterns of behavior are identifiable, but the transition process is quite individualized. Because the situation is complex, ever-changing and perennial, matches and mismatches between student and employer occur. During the past two decades, the problem has become a global issue because of high levels of youth unemployment. In Canada, large corporations and non-governmental organizations developed resource programs, in addition to government projects which are targeted more for disadvantaged groups. In addition, some good research has been conducted although little evaluation has been done. The resultant gradual consensus is that various skills will ease difficulties in the passage. Although these sets of skills overlap, they are not identical. In spite of all that has been accomplished, many youth do not receive sufficient support to navigate the transition successfully, given their abilities and education. Thus, more collaboration is required if society is to be renewed.

Megatrends that influence annual transitions include demographics, marketplace vagaries, gender differentiated career paths and public debt policies. Supply-demand pressures increase when the number of people competing for the same occupations is high. When youth apply for positions that also attract experienced adults displaced by corporate downsizing, they may not receive priority. Small to medium sized companies are growing, but they often are not involved in service relationships with youth and educational establishments. The profile of a woman's career cycle remains different from that of most men's, although the wage gap narrows at higher levels of employment; juggling professional and personal responsibilities during child bearing years is different for men and women, who still tend to have differing occupational interests. Governmental policies intervene to reduce disadvantages, but many youth fall between public support systems and the private sector service projects, while others receive assistance from multiple agencies without much observable progress.

Approximately 50% of youth experience an easy passage during this difficult and differentiated transition. A minority have ongoing personal and social problems that make them dependent upon assistance through their adult years. A few have bottleneck problems with educational systems, and some have transient lifestyles, and just pass through schools without becoming deeply involved in any. After time out, some adults re-enter intending to earn a post-secondary credential. Too few youths enter apprenticeship programs to meet labor market demands. Too many others flounder for lengthy periods, drifting aimlessly and underachieving. These latter categories could be reduced, thus increasing the numbers who navigate the transition more skillfully.

Part of the problem is that adult advisors are sequestered within either education or employment venues while the students are in passage. Therefore, informal networks such as family and friends become more influential when youth feel vulnerable, making decisions that may have negative consequences. Adults often mentor well but the timing may be poor. For example, high school students talk with teachers about further educational credentials, but are hesitant to use them for employment references.

Four types of skill sets assist youth to be more successful. They need meta-curricular skills to do well academically; they need job search skills to move from a student labor market to an adult one. They need job entry competencies to prove themselves and employability skills to develop a career path. Too frequently these constellations are presented as lists without guidance about how they may be integrated and used whenever they are needed. Skills need development and practise, but learning opportunities may be more *ad hoc* than planned.

Students and employers agree that educational credentials are important and the statistics confirm their perceptions that the investment pays off. A portfolio highlighting relevant part-time work experiences or volunteer activities benefits both prospective employees and the hiring team. Participation in service programs has reduced destructive blaming between educators and employers while teaching these adults about the complexities which affect the youth. However, an appreciation of the perennial nature of the issue is more slow. This problem cannot be solved by short-term projects. It requires commitment and collaboration from adult advisors or the financial and human wastage will not be effectively reduced.

Some matches and mismatches are inevitable in education-employment dynamics but the anxieties and patterns of behaviors of young people in transition are predictable. They need not be deterministic pitfalls that reduce the quality of life for an individual and erode society. Leaving school could be the most exciting part of adolescence: it is an opportunity to demonstrate talent and creativity, reflecting the vested aspirations of all concerned. All members of society have a concern that young people match their developing talents well to labor market dynamics.

References

Alberta Career Development and Employment (1992). *Employment status of 20-24 year olds enrolled in school, college or university, Alberta, 1977, 1980, 1985 & 1990*. Edmonton: author. January.

Alberta Intergovernmental Task Force (1994). *You Can Help – a school dropout information package*. Alberta Advanced Education and Career Development, Alberta Education, Alberta Family and Social Services, Alberta Health, Human Resource Development, Canada. Edmonton: author.

Axelrod, P. & Anisef, P. (1996). *Transitions, the life course, and the class of '73: Implications for social policy*. In B. Galaway & J. Hudson (Eds), *Youth in transition*. Toronto: Thompson Educational Publishing Inc. pp. 144-151.

Bowhay, C. (1994). *The school-to-work transition for disadvantaged youth in Calgary*. Calgary: Canada Employment Centre, Youth Employment Committee.

Cairns, K., Woodward, J. B. & Hashizume, L. (1992). Employment counsellors' and youths' views of the transition to work: Preparing to develop a work skills simulation. *Canadian Journal of Counselling, 26:4*. pp. 22-239.

Calgary Educational Partnerships Foundation (1996). *Employability skills: Creating my future workbook*. Toronto: Nelson Canada.

Calgary Educational Partnerships Foundation (CEPF) (1997). *PetroCanada School Resources Program, Business Caring for Students and Schools pamphlet*. Calgary: author.

Conference Board of Canada (1996). *100 best business-education partnerships idea book*. Toronto: author.

Conference Board of Canada (undated). *at a glance*. pamphlet, Toronto: author.

Conference Board of Canada / Catalyst (1997). *Closing the gap, women's advancement in corporate and professional Canada*. Toronto: author.

Corporate-Higher Education Forum (1997). *It pays to stay: Straight talk on getting and keeping good jobs*. Calgary: author.

Crysdale, S., Donaldson, E.L. & Joseph, S. (1987). *The Peel Pilot Study of Transition to Work: Youth, Parents, Teachers and Employers Speak out on Co-operative Education and Other Matters*. Toronto: York University, Sociology Department, SSHRC Grant Report.

Donaldson, E. L. (1995). Calgary's solution to the school-to-work transition, *Educational Leadership*, 52:8, pp.8-10. International Insert.

Donaldson, E. L. & Dixon, E. A. (1993). *First-year Chemistry student intentions and perceptions: Final report*. Calgary: University of Calgary, Faculty of Education.

Donaldson, E. L. (1992). Patterns and profiles in the transition from school to work. *Journal of Educational Administration and Foundations*, 7:1, pp. 30-48.

Evers, F, Rush, J., Krmpotic, J. & Duncan-Robinson, J. (1993). executive summary, *Making the Match: Phase III Final Technical Report*. Guelph: University of Guelph.

Foot, D. (1996). *Boom, bust & echo: How to profit from the coming demographic shift*. Toronto: Macfarlane, Walter & Ross.

Gaskell, J. (1992). *Gender matters from school to work*. Toronto: OISE Press.

Gilbert, S., Barr, L., Clark, W., Blue, M. & Sunter, D. (1993). *Leaving school*. Ottawa: Human Resources and Labour Canada.

Government of Canada (1993). *Leaving school: Results from a national survey comparing school leavers and high school graduates 18-20 years of age*. Ottawa: Human Resources and Labour Canada. September.

Government of Canda (1996). *The Class of 90 (A compendium of findings)* Ottawa: author.

Grayson, P. (1994). *Comparative first year experiences at York University: Science, Arts and Atkinson*. York University: Institute for Social Research.

Hiebert, B. & Tanner, G. (1995). *Student employability skills portfolio project evaluation report*. Calgary: Calgary Educational Partnerships Foundation.

Krahn, H & Lowe, G. (1998). *The 1997 Alberta graduate survey: Labour market and educational experiences of 1994 university graduates*. Edmonton: Alberta Advanced Eudcation and Career Development.

Logan, R. (1994). Voluntary part-time workers. *Perspectives*. Autumn, Ottawa: Statistics Canada, Catalogue 75-001E, pp.18-23.

Maxwell, J. (1992). *Economic Council of Canada presentation to the Conference Board of Canada's Business and Education Conference*. Ottawa: author.

O'Neil, J. (1991). Changing occupational structure. *Canadian social trends*. Ottawa: Statistics Canada. Winter, pp. 8-12.

Watt, D. & Roessingh, H. (1994). ESL Dropout: The myth of educational equity. *Alberta Journal of Educational Research. 60*:3, pp.283-296.

Chapter 5
Career Development and Self-Development: Features, Challenges and Resources

Michael C. Pyryt

Conceptualizing Career Development

This chapter views the process of career development as being intricately linked with the process of self-development. It is strongly influenced by Holland's (1973) theory of vocational choice and the literature on career education for the gifted (Frederickson, 1979; Hoyt & Hebeler, 1974; Rothney & Koopman, 1958; Sanborn, 1979). It is compatible with other models of career development such as developmental models (Super, 1981) and social learning models (Krumboltz, 1981). It focuses primarily on career development during adolescence. Cognitively, the emergence of formal operations (Inhelder & Piaget, 1958) enables adolescents to consider the many forces affecting career development. Affectively, the focus on identity issues (Erikson, 1950) during adolescence makes initial career and self-exploration particularly salient at this time. The following section will examine five ways to conceptualize careers: (a) Career as possibility, (b) Career as lifestyle, (c) Career as investment, (d) Career as mobility and (e) Career as innovation.

Career as Possibility

There are nearly 20 000 occupations listed in the *Dictionary of Occupation Titles* (United States Department of Labor, 1991). The number of possible careers is overwhelming. There are numerous structural models or maps that have been developed to classify occupations (Bizet & Carson, 1998). One important dimension for classifying occupations focuses on the aptitude required for occupational success. Another way to classify the world of work is in terms of interest clusters based on commonalities among occupations. Sophisticated maps that incorporate both aptitude and interest components have been developed (Gottfredson, 1986) and provide a useful schema for categorizing the world of work. Career choice is made easier when there is a narrow range of aptitude and interest. Career choice is made difficult by the combination of high intellectual aptitude and a wide range of interests. Many gifted students have the ability to succeed at many possible careers and strong interests in many areas. Imagine a student who is both talented and passionate about both quantum physics and classical music performance on instruments such as the violin. This student will have difficulties competing against others who devote their full energy to succeeding at either quantum physics or the violin. Early specialization is a correlate of eminent achievement (Bloom, 1985) There is a tendency for parents and teachers to put pressure on a child to specialize as soon as possible. Such pressure may create tension for the gifted individual. Parents and teachers need to patiently wait until the career path for a gifted child unfolds rather than prematurely forcing a career decision.

Career as Lifestyle

Each occupation entails a complete lifestyle that extends far beyond the role demands of a particular job. Some lifestyle considerations include: (a) the hours one works, (b) the clothes one wears, (c) the amount of travelling one does, (d) the amount of time spent with family, (e) the people one associates with and (f) types of recreational activities. Consider the lifestyle demands for a "typical" university professor. Although no clocks are punched, university professors often work 12-16 hour days to fulfill teaching, research and service requirements. Most university professors will spend significantly more money on membership in professional organizations than maintaining and enhancing their wardrobes. Professors regularly travel to conferences to present papers and network with colleagues. Professors must diligently protect their planned time with families. University professors can develop a diverse group of friends based on a diversity of avocational interests. Occupational satisfaction is likely to be affected by the compatibility between lifestyle demands of an occupation and the individual's lifestyle preferences. Individuals must identify their own lifestyle preferences as well as the lifestyle requirements of various occupations.

Career as Investment

The careers that many individuals aspire to require extensive educational preparation beyond the bachelor's degree. Such preparation often involves great financial and personal costs. Financially, one can always expect tuition fees to rise higher than the general rate of inflation. Personally, one spends additional years living the challenging life of a graduate student while one's friends may be prospering in their careers. The prolonged preparation time may complicate personal decisions regarding the timing of marriage and parenthood, since the demands of schooling are greatly complicated by family responsibilities. Due to socialization experiences and expectations, any decisions to defer child-rearing until some career goals are met will be more difficult for females than males. Due to assortative mating, the tendency to marry others of similar educational levels, the number of potential spouses decreases as one's educational level increases. Finding suitable employment in the same geographic locale becomes increasingly difficult when both spouses have highly specialized degrees.

Career as Mobility

Many individuals, particularly those from rural areas, aspire to occupations that will force them to leave their home community to seek training experiences and jobs. Even with access to the latest in internet-based coursework, a potential oceanographer from Ponoka, Alberta, would need to study in places such as Vancouver, San Diego or Miami to pursue a degree in oceanography. The need for geographic mobility may conflict with parental and cultural values that emphasize the precedence of family proximity over career choice. Parents may view a career in agriculture in the home community as preferable to a career in a major urban area 1000 kilometres away. Upward mobility in social class standing, which may accompany educational and occupational attainment, can lead to lifestyle changes that alienate an individual from one's home community. This alienation is magnified as exposure to diverse value systems due to geographic mobility decreases uncritical acceptance of the single systems in which one was raised. Frasier (1979) writes poignantly on the pain that upward mobility causes culturally diverse individuals.

Career as Innovation

Many currently-available career options are the direct result of the ingenuity of gifted individuals, who were able to "invent" their own careers. The field of astrophysics did not exist until someone combined interests in astronomy and physics. Individuals who want to combine several disciplines will require greater investments in content preparation than individuals who focus on a single discipline. The current fascination with computer-based technologies such as hypermedia will create many opportunities for individuals who can combine discipline-based expertise and technological skills. New occupations will be created through technological breakthroughs. Career development programs need to be flexible enough to empower individuals to invent their careers if they desire.

Self-Development in the Career Development Process

This section will describe important self-development skills that are intricately linked with career development. Although the components are presented sequentially, they are conceptualized as being interrelated and dynamically influencing each other.

Developing Awareness of Abilities and Interests

Students can make thoughtful career choices by developing awareness of aptitudes and interests. One of the easiest ways to make individuals aware of their aptitudes is through the use of multi-aptitude batteries such as the *Differential Aptitude Tests* (Bennett, Seashore & Wesman, 1982). Such instruments help an individual determine areas of strengths and weaknesses by providing a profile of cognitive abilities. For gifted students, the use of off-level testing enables students to get a clearer picture of their capabilities. The Talent Search model pioneered at The Johns Hopkins University (Cohn, 1991; Stanley, 1977) enables seventh graders to learn that without formal coursework they already outperform university-bound high school seniors on measures of scholastic aptitude. This experience helps students become aware of their vast potential. Using standardized personality inventories such as Holland's (1978) *Vocational Preference Inventory* can enhance self-awareness. This instrument, which is based on Holland's (1973) theory of vocational choice, categorizes occupations in terms of six personality types (realistic, investigative, artistic, social, enterprising and conventional). Realistic types prefer occupations that involve use of mechanical skills. Investigative types prefer occupations involving a search for the truth. Artistic types prefer occupations that promote creative expression. Social types prefer occupations that involve helping people. Enterprising types prefer occupations that encourage an entrepreneurial spirit. Conventional types prefer occupations that involve consistent routines. Results are interpreted in terms of personality type combinations found in various occupations. For example, the combination of social, artistic and investigative types are found most often among teachers of the gifted. Holland proposed that individuals are likely to be more satisfied when the careers they choose match their personalities. Although there are numerous career interest inventories available, an advantage of the Holland model is that it provides information to help individuals consider broad career areas compatible with interests rather than prematurely channelling them toward a single career. Other useful career interest inventories that can enhance self-awareness and be interpreted in relation to Holland's model include *The Self-Directed Search* (Holland, 1974) and the *Strong Interest Inventory* (Campbell & Hansen, 1985).

In addition to standardized tests, self-awareness can be developed through the use of informal questionnaires such as the Career Issues Survey. This instrument, which was used with gifted Australian high school students participating in a career development seminar at The University of New South Wales (Pyryt, 1996), explores students' reflections on issues such as multipotentiality, investment, lifestyle, mobility and expectations.

Developing an Awareness of Lifestyle Preferences

There are three techniques that can be beneficial in helping individuals become aware of lifestyle preferences. The first technique, personal reflection, which can be tapped through interviews, open-ended questionnaires or journals, involves having students respond to an open-ended question such as "Just suppose you were currently involved in your preferred occupation, describe what your life would be like." The second technique involves having the student interview individuals working in the students' occupational areas to determine what life is really like for the individual involved in a particular occupation. The third technique involves job shadowing or mentorship opportunities, where the student can more directly experience the lifestyle demands of a particular occupation. Sequential use of these techniques, having the students hypothesize about lifestyle demands, check their perceptions of the realities of those perceptions and directly experience these demands, will have a more powerful impact than use of the techniques in isolation.

Developing Awareness of External Barriers and Constraints

There are three major external barriers and constraints that individuals often have to cope with : expectations of others, costs and discrimination. The career expectations of significant others (parents, teachers and peers) can exert tremendous pressures for individuals. Families may differ in their valuing of higher education as a path to career success (Safter & Bruch, 1981).

Some may undervalue the benefits of higher education, particularly the need for study beyond the baccalaureate degree. They may actively discourage geographical mobility and strongly encourage commuting to the nearest institution of higher education. Some families will have exceedingly high expectations for their children. Family socialization practices may constantly expose children to the benefits of certain careers such as law or medicine. It is also likely that sex-role socialization leads to differential expectations about the appropriateness of various careers for males and females. Teachers may exert pressure for students to pursue careers in areas of teachers' interests. Peers may exert influences on which careers to pursue and locale for pursuing them.

As mentioned in the section on "Career as Investment," the cost of higher education continues to rise. Students may be overwhelmed by the financial commitment that baccalaureate and post-baccalaureate study will require. Honest discussion with parents regarding the balance of available family support and expected self-support will provide some sense of the financial resources needed for individuals to pursue their career dreams. A thorough understanding of the financial aid process and scholarship opportunities and requirements will help individuals compete for available resources. It is also possible to shorten the heavy time and financial sacrifices that professional aspirations require, by permitting individuals to accelerate their educational progress. The smorgasbord of educationally accelerative opportunities model pioneered by the Study of Mathematically Precocious Youth (SMPY) at The Johns Hopkins University provides much evidence for the effectiveness of accelerative practices, particularly in the areas of science and technology. Accelerative possibilities include early entrance to university, part-time university coursework, distance education, advanced placement, subject matter acceleration and grade skipping. The SMPY model has been replicated elsewhere. Other Universities operating projects based on the SMPY include: Duke University, Northwestern University, University of Denver, The University of Washington, Arizona State University, Iowa State University, the University of North Texas, Purdue University, Sacramento State University and the University of Wisconsin in Eau Claire (Stanley, 1991). Brody and Benbow (1987) have examined the effectiveness of the smorgasbord of opportunities model. Students who made use of accelerative options attended more selective universities, had higher university GPAs, won more university honors and had higher career aspirations than students who decided not to make use of these accelerative options.

Females and minority members may also have to cope with overt and covert sexism and racism as they pursue careers of their choice. Their talents may not be recognized and they may be counselled to pursue stereotypical and less-prestigious occupations than they desire. The best way for empowering individuals to cope with such discrimination is through the use of role models and mentorship experiences. Individuals from similar gender, racial and ethnic backgrounds who have successfully overcome these discriminatory barriers can serve as potential role models and mentors.

Developing Realistic Expectations of Career Requirements

There are two aspects to career development that students also need to learn: the necessary content preparation that is required to pursue and enter a discipline, and the commitment required for occupational success. Some students may underestimate the content preparation necessary to pursue areas of study. Sells (1980) has shown how mathematics serves as a critical filter to keep females from pursuing careers in mathematics and science. Some females opt out of mathematics courses at the earliest possible opportunity and find themselves with an insufficient mathematics background to major in the natural or social sciences. At some universities calculus is required to pursue a psychology major. Students may also fail to appreciate the training necessary to pursue careers of their choice. Minimally, a student needs to obtain a Master's degree in the Province of Alberta to practice as a chartered psychologist. Other provinces require a doctorate as the minimal level entry criterion.

Students may also not appreciate the truth in Edison's dictum that "Genius is 1% inspiration and 99% perspiration." They may expect eight hours of work and 16 hours of leisure. Sixteen hours of work and eight hours of leisure may be a more likely scenario. Pyryt (1993) has suggested "commitment bombardment" as a necessary technique for instilling an awareness of the absolute need for hard work in order to be successful. Exposure to successful adults both vicariously through biographies, autobiographies, and films and directly through role models and mentoring experiences is essential.

Developing Creative Problem-Solving Abilities

Training in creative problem-solving (CPS) can enable individuals to cope with the investment and mobility problems. The creative problem-solving process consists of the following steps: (a) fact-finding, (b) problem-finding, (c) idea-finding, (d) solution-finding and (e) acceptance-finding. During fact-finding, an individual non-judgmentally examines the parameters of the problem. During problem-finding, an individual brainstorms alternative problems that begin with the phrase, "In What Ways Might I" to try to capture the essence of what the problem really entails. During idea-finding, the individual brainstorms potential solutions to the core problem identified during problem-finding. During solution-finding an individual brainstorms criteria for judging the ideas and then evaluates ideas in relation to the criteria. During acceptance finding, the individual develops a plan of action for putting the idea into practice. CPS involves an oscillation between divergent thinking, a listing of many possible alternatives and convergent thinking, finding the correct answer. Numerous sources for teaching creative problem-solving are available (Cline, 1989; Feldhusen & Treffinger, 1985; Parnes, 1981, 1992; Treffinger & Isaksen, 1992). Training consists of guided practice through each of the steps until the process is internalized and can be independently applied.

Developing Interpersonal Skills for Career Success

It is important to develop an effective style of communicating since skills in interacting with others are more related to occupational success than general intellectual ability (Goleman, 1995). Competent communicators effectively use the skills of self-disclosure, empathy, warmth, social relaxation, assertiveness, interaction management, descriptiveness, sensitivity to feelings, flexibility and relationship stage skills (Friedman, 1978a). These particular skills are multi-faceted and context-dependent. For example, there are several classes of assertive behavior: giving and receiving compliments, initiating interactions, requesting a change in behavior, and resisting pressure from others which are expressed in the context of interacting with family members, friends, acquaintances, authority figures, strangers, service personnel. An individual might be able to assertively initiate a conversation with an acquaintance, but have difficulty asking a stranger to refrain from smoking. There are various models for interpersonal skills development that have evolved in the disciplines of speech communications and human relations (Bochner & Kelly, 1974; Giffin & Patton, 1974; Friedman, 1978b) and counsellor training (Carkhuff, 1969). The essential features of these approaches involve didactic instruction regarding the nature of the behavior, modelling the appropriate verbal and non-verbal expression of the behavior, client rehearsal of the behavior in role-play and simulated settings with trainer coaching and feedback, and implementation of the behavior in real-world settings. These approaches can be applied to help individuals use interpersonal communication skills effectively in the communication contexts that they will face.

Developing Strategies for Overcoming Arbitrary Sex-role Stereotyping

Special effort should be made to eliminate arbitrary sex-role stereotyping (Fox, Brody & Tobin, 1980; Fox, Tobin & Brody, 1981; Gutek, 1979). Wolleat (1979) advocated the use of such techniques as direct communication and education on the negative impact of sex-role stereotyping, career decision-making simulations, exposure to role models, formation of support groups and same-sex career days to combat negative effects of sex-role stereotyping. Developing a positive expectation regarding perceived success in future careers is also important (Eccles & Harold, 1992). One technique for encouraging reflective thinking about life planning is called "Lifeline." Students draw a line representing their life from birth to perceived time of death. They indicate their current placement and future milestones along the line. If a child's line reflects traditional patterns such as education, marriage, raising a family without career involvement, the child is asked to consider possible scenarios such as death of spouse or divorce. Visioning such scenarios enables students to develop a healthy respect for the complexities of life and the need to keep options open. Although typically discussed in the context of encouraging women to pursue careers in mathematics and science, special efforts also need to be made to encourage males to explore careers in the arts and teaching at the primary level.

Development Strategies for Coping with Stress and Managing Time

As with other life transitions (see Chapter 3 of this volume) stress management strategies can help individuals cope with the career development problems of investment, mobility and expectations. Stress can be alleviated through progressive relaxation (Jacobson, 1939), breathing techniques (Wenger, 1979), imagery techniques (Samuels & Samuels, 1975) and environmental sounds (Rosenfeld, 1979). Exposure to a variety of techniques is necessary to enable individuals to determine for themselves the stress management technique(s) used singly or in combination that they find most useful. Time management strategies (Ferner, 1980; Lakein, 1980; Zucker, 1980) can help students set priorities and begin to make choices.

Developing Career Self-Efficacy

One needs a positive self-image to cope with the expectations, investment demands and mobility factors that high aspirations entail. Numerous materials have been developed to enhance self-concept (Treffinger, Borgers, Render & Hoffman, 1976; Karnes & Collins, 1980). Pyryt & Mendaglio (1996/1997) have introduced a theory-driven approach to assessing and enhancing self-concept. This instrument, called the **Pyryt Mendaglio Self-Perception Survey (PMSPS)**, examines academic, social, physical ability, physical appearance and ethical self-concept from three theoretical perspectives: reflected appraisals, social comparison and attribution. Examination of responses in conjunction with a follow-up interview leads to a unique plan for enhancing self-concept. Interventions from a reflected appraisals perspective involve examining the accuracy of perceptions of the evaluations of significant others. Interventions from the social comparison perspective involve examining the characteristics of the reference group for social comparisons and encouraging success experiences. Interventions from the attribution perspective involve encouraging individuals to make ability attributions through successful accomplishment of challenging experiences. It's hard for successful Talent Search participants, who as seventh graders perform better than university-bound high school seniors on measures of scholastic aptitude, to attribute their success to luck, ease of test or simply hard work.

These same theoretical models can be used to understand the development of career self-efficacy or the belief that one will succeed at a chosen occupation. The reflected appraisals approach suggests that individuals develop a career self-concept by their perceptions of the evaluations of significant others. When parents, teachers and peers comment on areas that individuals show talent or note potential areas for career success, individuals filter these comments a positive self-scheme ("Everyone says I'm good at Math and would make a good mathematician"). In school, social comparison processes operate and individuals directly compare their achievement with others'. ("I get the highest marks in Math; Compared to others I can be successful mathematician"). In heterogeneous educational settings, bright students may develop inflated self-concepts as Big-Fishes-in-Little-Ponds eventually to become Little-Fishes-In-Big-Ponds when they enter universities. Eventually, they make attributions or explanations for their success ("I do well on Math tests because I am good at Math; I will do well as a mathematician because I am good at Math"). This process is reinforced as individuals succeed at their chosen occupations.

Resources for Integrating Self-Development and Career Development

This section describes some resources that might help individuals learn more about self-development and career development processes. It includes a discussion of the role of helping professionals, print-based resources and computer-based resources. The list of resources is necessarily illustrative rather than comprehensive.

Educational and Guidance Personnel

One effective way of linking self-development and career development is through a structured career development program offered by a trained professional. The first component of the program would be an assessment of abilities, career interests and values. The second component would focus on developing an understanding of the nature of the world of work and provide opportunity to acquire some basic information regarding occupations: discussion of the nature of an occupation, educational preparation needed to enter a particular occupation, potential salary ranges for those involved in the occupation, outlook for the future. The third component would involve direct placement at a work site through some internship, mentorship or apprenticeship program. The fourth component would focus on some basic job-hunting skills such as locating potential career opportunities, developing exemplary cover letters and résumés, and presenting oneself favorably in an interview. A school counsellor would be best suited to implement such a program. Given limited budgets for helping professionals in schools and other demands on the school counsellor's time, educators with varied competencies will often be responsible for implementing such a program.

Selected Print-Based Resources

One of the most popular and comprehensive sources of information regarding careers and the career development process is *What Color is Your Parachute?* by Richard Bolles (1998), which is updated yearly and available at any local bookstore. The book is a compendium of informal self-assessment techniques, sources for information about careers, and sources for job-hunting skills. Another interesting book also from Bolles (1978) is *The Three Boxes of Life and How to get Out of Them*. This work focuses on the preferred distribution of learning, work and leisure in one's life and developing plans for ensuring that one's actual life experience in these areas is congruent with one's preferred distribution. The *Occupational Outlook Handbook 1998-1999* published by the United States Department of Labor provides descriptive information and projections about the viability of over 1000 careers. *Making Vocational Choices: A Theory of Vocational Choices and Work Environments* is the latest volume by John Holland, which describes his theory of vocational choice and provides references to the most current research on the model.

Selected Internet Resources

There is a overwhelming amount of information available on the Internet regarding career development. If one has no particular website in mind, the starting place would be www.yahoo.com, a popular search to vocational education and career education sites. If one wanted to acquire some of the books described in the previous section or find out if there were any books available on careers in psychology, one could go to www.amazon.com, the largest bookstore on the Internet. Professionals seeking syntheses of the latest research on career development can go to coe.ohio-state.edu/cete/ericacve/index.html, the ERIC Clearinghouse on Adult, Career and Vocational Education (ERIC/ACVE) located at the Center on Education and Training (CETE) at The Ohio State University. This site provides access to ERIC digests in the areas of career education (childhood through adult), adult and continuing education, and vocational and technical education including employment and training. The University of Alberta has numerous links through its Career and Placement Services (www.ualberta.ca/~caps) website. Their current monthly "hotsites" has links to 34 websites dealing with all aspects of career planning and work search. Their Canadian Job Postings and Databases link provides an annotated list of 20 websites for job postings across Canada ranging from the Globe and Mail at www.careers.theglobeandmail.com to Human Resources Development Canada office in Calgary at www.ffa.ucalgary.ca, which provides access to the labor market and career information with links to the Calgary Job Bank and Calgary Hire-a-Student office. The Canadian Jobs and Employment Catalogue at www.kenevacorp.mb.ca provides "Canadian Only" access to job banks, resume creation sites, job interview sites, occupation specific sites and employment classifieds among its sites. For an Alberta perspective, Advanced Education and Career Development located at www.aecd.gov.ab.ca provides information on career and educational options in Alberta and links to other resources.

Summary

This chapter attempted to examine some of the key features of career development organized along the themes of Career as Possibility, Career as Lifestyle, Career as Investment, Career as Mobility and Career as Innovation. Several self-development processes were identified as intricately linked to career development. One set of processes focuses on awareness of abilities, interests, lifestyle preferences, career requirements, and external barriers/constraints. Another set of processes involves skill based training in creative problem-solving, interpersonal effectiveness, gender empowerment, stress/time management and career self-efficacy. Although presented linearly, the career development features and self-development processes are viewed as working interactively. Basic components of a structured career development program are provided together with selected print and Internet-based resources.

References

Bizot, E. H. & Carson, A. D. (1998, April). *Theory of the Occupation Aptitude Patterns (OAP) Map and Its Relations to Other Structural Models of Occupations*. Paper presented at the meeting of the American Educational Research Association, San Diego.

Bloom, B.S. (1985) (Ed.). *Developing talent in young people*. New York: Ballantine.

Bochner, A. P. & Kelly, C. W. (1974). Interpersonal competence: Rationale, philosophy, and implementation of a conceptual framework. *The Speech Teacher, 23*, 279-301.

Brody, L. E. & Benbow, C. P. (1987). Accelerative practices: How effective are they for the gifted? *Gifted Child Quarterly, 31*, 105-110.

Bolles, R. N. (1978). *The three boxes of life and how to get out of them: An introduction to life-work planning*. Berkeley, CA: Ten Speed Press.

Bolles, R. N. (1998). *The 1998 what color is your parachute?: A practical guide for job-hunters and career changers*. Berkeley, CA: Ten Speed Press.

Hansen, J. C. & Campbell, D. P. (1985). *Manual for the Strong Interest Inventory*. (4th Edition). Stanford, CA: Stanford University Press.

Carkhuff, R. R. (1969). *Helping and human relations: A primer for lay and professional helpers* (Vol 2). New York: Holt, Rinehart & Winston.

Cline, S. (1989). *What would happen if I said yes?...A guide to creativity for parents and teachers*. East Aurora, NY: D.O.K Publishers.

Cohn, S. J. (1991). Talent searches. In N. Colangelo & G. A. Davis (Eds.), *Handbook of gifted education* (pp. 166-177). Needham Heights, MA: Allyn & Bacon.

Eccles, J. & Harold, R. D. (1992). Gender differences in educational and occupational patterns among the gifted. In N. Colangelo, S. G. Assouline & D. L. Ambroson (Eds.), *Talent development: Proceedings from the 1991 Henry B. and Jocelyn Wallace National Research Symposium on Talent Development*. Unionville, NY: Trillium Press.

Erikson, E. (1951). *Childhood and society*. New York: Norton.

Feldhusen, J. F. & Treffinger, D. J. (1985). *Creative thinking and problem solving in gifted education* (3rd ed.). Dubuque, IA: KendallHunt.

Ferner, J. D. (1980). *Successful time management*. New York: Wiley.

Foster, W. (1982). Self-concept, intimacy, and the attainment of excellence. *Journal for the Education of the Gifted, 6*, 20-29.

Fox, L. H., Brody, L. & Tobin, D. (Eds.). (1980). *Women and the mathematical mystique*. Baltimore: The Johns Hopkins University Press.

Fox, L. H., Tobin, D. & Brody, L. (1981). Career development of gifted and talented women. *Journal of Career Education, 7*, 289-298.

Frasier, M. M. (1979). Counseling the culturally diverse gifted. In N. Colangelo & R. T. Zaffrann (Eds.), *New voices in counseling the gifted* (pp. 304-311). Dubuque, IA: Kendall-Hunt.

Frederickson, R. H. (1979). Career development and the gifted. In N. Colangelo & R.T. Zaffrann (Eds.), *New voices in counseling the gifted* (pp. 264-276). Dubuque, IA: Kendall-Hunt.

Friedman, P. G. (1978a, November). *Social giftedness: Description and development.* Paper presented at the meeting of the National Association for Gifted Children, Houston.

Friedman, P. G. (1978b). *Interpersonal communications: Innovations in instruction.* Washington, DC: National Education Association.

Giffin, K. & Patton, B. R. (1974). *Personal communication in human relations.* Columbus, OH: Merrill.

Goleman, D. P. (1993). *Emotional intelligence: Why it can matter more than IQ for character, health and lifelong achievement.* New York: Bantam Books.

Gottfredson, L. S. (1986). Occupational Aptitude Patterns Map: Development and implications for a theory of job aptitude requirements [Monograph]. *Journal of Vocational Behavior, 29,* 254-291.

Gutek, B. A. (Ed.). (1979). *Enhancing women's career development.* San Francisco: Jossey-Bass.

Holland, J. L. (1973). *Making vocational choices: A theory of careers.* Englewood Cliffs, NJ: Prentice-Hall.

Holland, J. L. (1974). *The Self-Directed Search: A guide to educational and vocational planning.* Palo Alto, CA: Consulting Psychologists Press.

Holland, J. L. (1978). *Vocational Preference Inventory manual.* Palo Alto, CA: Consulting Psychologists Press.

Holland, J. L. (1997). *Making vocational choices: A theory of vocational personalities and work environments* (3rd. Ed.). Odessa, FL: Psychological Assessment Resources.

Hoyt, K. B. & Hebeler, J. R. (Eds.). (1974). *Career education for gifted and talented students.* Salt Lake City: Olympus.

Inhelder, B. & Piaget, J. (1958). *The growth of logical thinking from childhood to adolescence.* New York: Basic Books.

Jacobson, E. (1938). *Progressive relaxation.* Chicago: University of Chicago Press.

Karnes, F. A. & Collins, E. C. (1980). *Handbook of instructional resources and references for teaching the gifted.* Boston: Allyn & Bacon.

Krumboltz, J. D. (1981). A social learning theory of career selection. In D. H. Montross & C. J. Shinkman (Eds.), *Career development in the 80's: Theory and practice* (pp. 43-66). Springfield, IL: Thomas.

Lakein, A. (1973). *How to get control of your time and your life.* New York: Wyden.

Parnes, S. J. (1981). *The magic of your mind.* Buffalo: Creative Education Foundation.

Parnes, S. J. (Ed.). (1992). *Source book for creative problem-solving.* Buffalo: Creative Education Foundation Press.

Pyryt, M. C. (1993). The three faces of creativity revisited: Intimacy, passion, and commitment. *Gifted Education International, 9*(3), 22-23.

Pyryt, M. C. (1996, January). *Charting your course.* Presented at Career development Seminar, University of New South Wales.

Pyryt, M. C. & Mendaglio, S. (1996/1997). The many facets of self-concept: Insights from the Pyryt Mendaglio Self-Perception Survey. *Exceptionality Education Canada, 6*(2), 75-83.

Rosenfeld, E. (1973). *The book of highs: 250 ways to alter consciousness without drugs.* New York: Quadrangle.

Rothney, J. W. M. & Koopman, N. E. (1958). Guidance of the gifted. In N. B. Henry (Ed.), *Education for the gifted: The fifty-seventh yearbook of the National Society for the Study of Education* (pp. 347-361). Chicago: National Society for the Study of Education.

Safter, H. T. & Bruch, C. B. (1981). Use of the DGG model for differential guidance of the gifted. *Gifted Child Quarterly, 25,* 167-174.

Samuels, M. & Samuels, N. (1975). *Seeing with the mind's eye: The history, techniques, and uses of visualization.* New York: Random House.

Sanborn, M. P. (1979). Counseling and guidance needs of the gifted and talented. In A. H. Passow (Ed.), *The gifted and talented: Their education and development.* (pp. 424-438). Chicago: National Society for the Study of Education.

Sells, L. W. (1980). The mathematics filter and the education of women and minorities. In L. H. Fox, L. Brody & D. Tobin (Eds.), *Woman and the mathematical mystique* (pp.66-75). Baltimore: The Johns Hopkins University press.

Stanley, J. C. (1977). Rationale of the Study of Mathematically Precocious Youth (SMPY) during its first five years of promoting educational acceleration. In J. C. Stanley, W. C. George & C. H. Solano (Eds.), *The gifted and the creative: A fifty-year perspective* (pp. 75-112). Baltimore: The Johns Hopkins University Press.

Stanley, J. C. (1991). An academic model for educating the mathematically talented. *Gifted Child Quarterly, 35,* 36-42.

Super, D. E. (1981). A develpmental theory: Implementing a self-concept. In D. H. Montross & C. J. Shinkman (Eds.), *Career development for the 1980s: Theory and practice* (pp. 28-42). Springfield, IL: Thomas.

Treffinger, D. J., Borgers, S. B., Render, G. F. & Hoffman, R. M. (1976). Encouraging affective development: A compendium of techniques and resources. *Gifted Child Quarterly, 20,* 47-65.

Treffinger, D. J. & Isaksen, S. (1992). *Creative problem solving: An introduction.* Sarasota, FL: Center for Creative Learning.

United States Department of Labor (1991). *Dictionary of occupational titles* (4th ed.). Washington, DC: US Government Printing Office.

United States Department of Labor (1998). *The Occupations outlook handbook 1998-1999.* Chicago: Bureau of Labor Statistics.

Wenger, W. (1979). *Beyond OK: Psychegenic tools relating to health of mind and body.* Gaithersburg, MD: Psychegenics Press.

Wolleat, P. (1979). Guiding the career development of gifted females. In N. Colangelo & R. T. Zaffrann (Eds.), *New voices in counseling the gifted* (pp. 331-345). Dubuque, IA: KendallHunt.

Zuker, E. (1980). *The successful woman's guide to time management.* Winston-Salem, NC: L'Eggs Products.

Chapter 6
Anticipating Milestone Transitions

Michael C. Pyryt and Bryan Hiebert

Overview

The purpose of this chapter is to discuss several common life transitions. Although the transitions of educational preparation, career involvement, relationship development and parenting are presented in separate sections, it is essential to recognize that these life cycle events occur simultaneously and dynamically affect each other. Consider the example of an elementary teacher who is pursuing a Master's Degree in Educational Leadership to have a credential needed to become an elementary principal. As a working professional, this individual spends two nights a week attending classes at the university and most weekends completing assignments. If courses are available in Spring and Summer sessions, the individual would be able to complete the degree in two years. A less intense pace would require three-to-four years. Job demands would affect opportunity for graduate study. The rigor of graduate study would affect the ability to cope with job demands. The situation is further complicated when the individual is a parent, since parenting responsibilities may conflict with job demands and graduate study requirements. A supportive spouse or partner might alleviate some of the stress related to the parenting role. Unless one is careful, the relationship might suffer if the spouse/partner feels that he or she is being neglected. Relationship challenges will affect parenting behavior, job performance and graduate pursuits. This simple scenario is repeated daily for numerous teachers across Canada and such problems are not restricted to professional educators. This chapter is written in the hopes that it will empower individuals to cope with the transitions that they are likely to face.

Negotiating the Educational Maze

One transition that has multiple transition points is the degree of educational attainment. Although there are multiple ways to characterize educational attainment (Hollingshead & Redlich, 1958), this section addresses four educational transitions: less than high school, high school diploma, baccalaureate degree, graduate degree.

Less Than High School

On April 14, 1998, Statistics Canada released information from the 1996 census regarding trends in education, mobility and migration on its daily news website (www.statcan.ca/Daily/English/980414/d980414.html). The data indicate that 35% of the Canadian population aged 15 and over in 1996 had not completed high school, a 13% improvement from the 48% of aged 15 and over in 1981 who had not completed high school. In 1996, 79% of the population aged 15-19 were attending school on a full-time basis, compared to 66% of those aged 15-19 in 1981. About 18% of the Canadian population aged 20-29 had less than a high school diploma in 1996.

Data were also reported in terms of unemployment rates for those aged 25-34. Compared to the unemployment rate of 4.6% for university graduates, the unemployment rate for persons 25-34 with less than a high school diploma was 18%. A more optimistic look at these statistics suggests that 82% of Canadians aged 25-34 made a transition to the labor force. Unfortunately, the brief report does not present information regarding income level and occupational status by level of educational attainment.

Individuals who choose to terminate their educational pursuits before obtaining a high school diploma will need opportunities for career exploration and vocational training. Ideally, they will have the opportunity to engage in a meaningful workplace experience before making the determination that they view entering the workforce as more rewarding than staying in school. The transition is most likely to be successful when three factors occur: (a) one's chosen occupation does not require an educational credential; (b) one has the necessary cognitive and affective skills to be successful in one's career and (c) one is passionate about one's chosen occupation.

High School Diploma

According to the 1996 census report, over three million Canadians aged 15 and over have a high school diploma as their terminal degree. Some individuals may choose to terminate their educational careers upon receiving a high school diploma. This choice may be forced upon them when access to institutions of higher education is not a viable option. In Alberta, for example, entrance to university is determined by performance in particular high school courses. The University of Calgary typically requires four core subjects to be taken at the highest curricular level and a composite achievement level of 70% for a student to be admitted. Students who graduate from high school without the requisite course sequence or required standard will not be admitted. In the United States, access to higher education is increased through the use of entrance examinations. High scores on measures such as the Scholastic Aptitude Tests can compensate for low GPAs. Thus, the transition process at the high school diploma level will differ depending on whether or not individuals make a conscious choice to terminate their formal educational pursuits at this level or find themselves unable to access higher education. If one makes the choice to terminate one's educational preparation at the high school level, transitional planning will focus on career and vocational training in much the same manner as for those who leave high school early. Matching aptitudes, interests and educational background will be the key to helping individuals make successful transitions to the world of work. If one is unable to immediately access an institution of higher education due to low GPA, transitional planning will focus on developing a plan for meeting the entrance requirements at one's preferred college or university. This plan is likely to involve additional coursework at the high school level or equivalent, either on-site or through distance education. Part of the training should consist of enhancing individuals' learning strategies and study skills, so that they can be more effective at organizing information for memory storage and retrieval. Training in test-wiseness would also be beneficial since it would enable individuals to enhance their test performance and increase grades.

University Degree

Another transition affecting numerous Canadians (over three million) is the initial university degree. The transition from high school to university is filled with challenges and opportunities. Academically, the university provides intellectual challenges. Students are typically responsible for mastering 30-50 pages of material in each subject each week. Unlike high school, where there are frequent quizzes and other opportunities to demonstrate knowledge, students in universities are typically given a limited number of opportunities (Mid-Term, Final, Research Paper) to demonstrate content mastery. Due to the competitive admissions standards, classes in universities will be more homogenous than high school classes. Academic achievers who were "Big-Fishes-in-Little-Ponds" in high school now find themselves "Little-Fishes in-Big-Ponds" in universities. Students may have the devastating experience of working harder than ever and earning their lowest composite GPA. Some university students might be residing away from home for the first time in their lives. Although this arrangement fosters independence and self-discipline, some students have difficulties coping with the freedom. They may spend more time partying than studying and their grades will reflect this choice. Financial obligations may require part-time employment which will also affect study plans. University experience presents the opportunity to pursue rigorous academic work. It provides an intellectually-stimulating environment with exposure to professors who are experts in their content domain and to intelligent peers.

The transition to university is enhanced by thoughtful selection of the university to attend. A potential student should ensure that the university offers the academic program that fits the student's abilities, interests and career goals. For many students the social environment that a university provides will be an important determinant of enjoyment of the university experiment. Besides reading university calendars, potential students should plan visits to the school during the academic term. Proximity to home and size of school will be important variables to consider. The cost of the university and one's ability to finance that cost will be a major consideration in university selection. Once selected and admitted, issues such as educational preparation, note-taking skills, study skills, test-taking skills and stress/time-management skills will affect individual success at university.

One decision that university students will make is whether they will enter the world of work after receiving their baccalaureate degree or whether they will continue to pursue Master's or Doctoral degrees or other forms of post-baccalaureate study such as Medicine. If one chooses to enter the world of work after receiving the baccalaureate degree, transition planning will focus on career planning and self-presentation skills through resume development and interview skills training. If the decision is to continue one's studies, transitional planning will involve identifying potential graduate schools, determining admission requirements, preparing for and completing any examinations (*Graduate Record Examinations, Law School Admissions Test, Medical Colleges Admissions Test*), and completing application forms. Typically, application forms require submission of transcripts, personal statements, curriculum vitae and letters of recommendation. The value of letters of recommendation written by professors is that they are mentors who can comment on a student's personal characteristics and accomplishments. Students can increase the possibility of finding potential mentors through succeeding at upper level (lower enrolment courses) and conducting independent research under the supervision of a professor. Students can increase their opportunities for such options if they enter universities with Advanced Placement or International Baccalaureate credits so they can immediately begin to specialize in their chosen areas.

Post-Baccalaureate Degrees

The graduate experience parallels the undergraduate experience with a few wrinkles. The workload at the graduate level will be more intensive with research papers replacing tests as the typical indicator of content mastery. Unless the program is totally course-based, students will need to complete a thesis, which they will defend in an Oral Examination. As a culminating experience, the thesis process involves steps such as selection of problem and proposed methodology, approval by supervisor or supervisory committee, approval by University Ethics Committee, permission for data collection, implementation of data collection activities, data analysis and interpretation, approval of written document and oral defense. For many students the thesis will be the most scrutinized piece of writing of their lives. In addition to the academic rigors, financial pressures will be intensified for many students since they will likely receive less, if any, financial support from their parents.

Facilitating the transitions at graduate level involve refining problem-solving skills, time/stress management skills, and written and oral communication skills. In completing a thesis, unhealthy perfectionism may lead to procrastination. Part of the transition process may involve helping students recognize the difference between enabling perfectionism, the striving to do one's best, from disabling perfectionism, the inability to do anything because whatever one does won't be perfect (Bransky, Jenkins-Friedman & Murphy, 1987). Training in career planning and self-presentation skills in letters of application, curriculum vitae preparation and interview skills will enhance opportunities for employment in one's chosen field.

Negotiating the Career Maze

Another major life transition is the choice of and entry into a career. Issues related to entry into the career have been discussed extensively in Chapter 5 of this volume. Individuals must deal with issues such as career possibilities, investment requirements, lifestyle preferences, mobility, expectations and unpredictability in evaluating potential careers. They are aided by self-awareness of abilities and interests, creative problem-solving, interpersonal skills, time/stress management skills and positive self-concepts. This section assumes that individuals have completed the necessary educational preparations and are ready for their first job.

Growing into a Career

Once a person accepts an offer of employment informally through a handshake, or formally through a written contract, the individual begins an important phase in their lives known as the transition to the world of work. This transition, which will typically involve 25-40 years of one's life for the individual with at least a baccalaureate degree, can take a variety of patterns. The notion is that someone with a BA at 22 probably will work 40 years before retiring. Some with a Ph.D. at 30 will work 25-35 years, depending upon age-of-retirement. Using the teaching profession as example, some teachers may stay with the same school jurisdiction from initial hiring until retirement. Other teachers might work for several different school jurisdictions over the course of their careers. Another group of teachers might work in one or more school jurisdictions, then change careers and work as trainers in the corporate world.

Upon entering a profession, one typically undergoes a probationary period. In industry, this probationary period may last six months to a year. In academia, the probationary period typically lasts six years. During the probationary period, the individual grows from novice to accomplished professional. In academia, this involves demonstrating excellence in research, teaching and service. In the research area, one must develop and implement a productive research program. Such a program involves the ability to conduct research and to communicate the results in presentations and publications. The ability to secure external funding to support the research program facilitates research productivity. In the teaching area, one must design and deliver courses. Course design elements include decisions related to the content to be covered, readings to be assigned and evaluation system to be used. Course delivery involves implementation of instructional activities, which typically involve some combination of lecture, discussion and student activities. In the service area, one must contribute to the functioning of the university by serving on departmental, faculty and university committees and contribute to the discipline through involvement with discipline-based organizations. One of the learning processes for a new faculty member is to learn the types of activities in each of the areas that are most valued. Unless one is careful, one can spend vast amounts of time serving on a committee that yields limited intrinsic or extrinsic benefits. Time management skills are essential as faculty members must prioritize competing research, teaching and service demands. It is also important to develop positive relationships with colleagues. Ideally, a newly-appointed assistant professor will soon find a senior scholar to serve as a mentor, who will provide guidance and support as the novice learns the ropes of the profession. In academia, a yearly review process provides feedback regarding the progress an individual is making in the areas of research, teaching and service. The probationary period culminates with the granting of tenure. This status enables the individual to pursue controversial research issues without fear of reprisals from the administration. Although the faculty member still has expectations regarding research, teaching and service, tenure provides a certain degree of job security, except in times of financial exigency. The other milestones for an academic are the promotions from assistant professor to associate professor and from associate professor to full professor. Each rank has increasing expectations regarding research, teaching and service. From a transitions point of view, the major components include ensuring that the educational preparation provides the content background for research and teaching, developing interpersonal communication skills to facilitate collaboration with colleagues, developing time management skills to prioritize competing demands, developing stress management skills to cope with the variety of stressors and developing self-confidence that one will be successful in the areas of research, teaching and service. The areas of content knowledge, interpersonal communications skills, time management skills, stress management skills and self-confidence will facilitate the transition to the world of work, regardless of the career path chosen.

Negotiating the Relationship Maze

Another transition that will affect most individuals is the development of an intimate relationship with another person. Relationships, like careers, can take many patterns. This section highlights some basic understandings from the "psychology of love."

Triangulating Love

Sternberg (1986, 1988) has developed a triangular theory of love. It has three basic components: intimacy, passion and commitment. Intimacy refers to one's ability to interact in a warm, caring manner and share feelings with the other person. Passion refers to the physical dimensions of relationships. Commitment refers to both the decision to have a long-term relationship and the perseverance to maintain the relationship. Each of these components contributes to the type of relationship experience. A relationship with only intimacy as a feature is characterized as a providing a true friendship, marked by feelings of closeness and warmth toward the other person without intense passion or long term commitment. A relationship marked only by passion is predicted to have a short term duration since infatuated love leads to an idealized view of the other not mirrored in reality, tends to be obsessive and tends to be asymmetrical. A relationship with only commitment present will be stable but dreary. The combination of intimacy and passion leads to a romantic loving relationship that will last a brief period of time, such as over the summer. The combination of intimacy and commitment leads to compassionate love, a deep caring for the other person found in marriages where the partners are each other's best friend. The combination of passion and commitment leads to fatuous love, in which the initial attraction and decision for commitment cannot compensate for the lack of intimacy. The combination of intimacy, passion and commitment leads to consummate or complete love. Each partner has their own perception of the triangles depicting their relationship. Greater congruity in perceptions is correlated with greater satisfaction in the relationship (Sternberg & Barnes, 1985). The components are viewed as dynamically interacting and influencing each other.

These components can provide some insights in terms of the transition to relationship development. In terms of intimacy, the major skills that need to be developed are interpersonal communication skills. Interaction management or the ability to keep conversations going smoothly (Wiemann, 1977) is one of the components leading to the development of intimacy. The substance of the conversation or the degree of self-disclosure (Jourard, 1971) is also critical. Disclosure in relationships typically proceeds from superficial to more intimate in a reciprocal manner (Altman & Taylor, 1973). The ability to express one's feelings and to respond sensitively to the feelings of others is another key interpersonal communication skill (Friedman, 1978) leading to the development of intimacy. Passion has strong physiological components (Leibowitz, 1983) as well as cognitive, emotional and behavioral components (Hatfield, 1988). Cognitive components include preoccupation with the partner, idealization of the partner and the desire to know all about the partner. Emotional components include attraction, desire for union, positive feelings when things go well, negative feelings when things go poorly, physiological arousal and a longing for reciprocity. Behavioral components include actions to support and make the other person happy, looking for signs of the other's feelings and studying the other person. An individual can use these signs to gauge the intensity of the passion component. The best preparation for developing the decision to have a long term relationship and the perseverance to maintain the relationship is the good fortune of having one's parents as role models who have successfully maintained their relationship. Wallerstein (1986) notes the difficulty that children of divorced parents experience in forming and maintaining relationships. The two components that seem to facilitate relationship maintenance are the willingness to work on the relationship and a sense of relationship efficacy, that the relationship will succeed.

Enhancing/Maintaining Relationships

Branden (1988) provides some of the behaviors that are characteristic of successful couples, who remain happily in love over a long period of time. The first behavioral component is verbal expression of love, which nurtures feelings of love. Successful couples tend to be physically affectionate and hand-holding, kissing, hugging and cuddling. Successful couples express their love sexually as a way to communicate their love and caring. They use mutual self-disclosure to reveal more of themselves to each other. Successful couples provide each other with an emotional support system, which nurtures each's well-being. Successful couples use gifts to bring joy to their partner's faces. They recognize that their partner's virtues outweigh their shortcomings. The final behavioral component identified by Branden is that successful couples make time to be alone together. Branden (1988) views the capacity to have a successful relationship dependent upon high self-esteem and courage. The behaviors described are quite consistent with the intimacy, passion and commitment components of Sternberg's (1986, 1988) triangular theory of love.

Negotiating the Parenting Maze

Another life event that many individuals will experience is parenting. This transition typically begins with the confirmation that a child has been conceived and ends when one breathes one's last breath. This section will highlight some of the major tasks of development, paying special attention to Erickson's (1950) stages of personality development and focus on parenting behaviors.

The First Five Years

The first psychological challenge for a newborn is to determine whether the external world is likely to provide a safe and secure physical and emotional environment. The challenge for parents is to help the child develop a sense of trust rather than a sense of mistrust about the world. The primary caretaker, typically the natural mother, has the most impact in helping the child find the world a safe place. The mother promotes this sense of security through responsiveness to the child's cries. There is a reciprocal interaction pattern between mother and child, such that the temperament of the child affects responsiveness and responsiveness affects the temperament of a child (Ainsworth, Bell & Stayton, 1974). Between 6 months and 18 months, the child demonstrates a bond with the mother known as an attachment (Ainsworth, 1964) which is marked by differential smiling and vocalization in the presence of the mother and separation anxiety when the child becomes aware that the mother is absent. The security of the initial attachment forms the basis for subsequent attachments (Bowlby, 1971). In two parent homes, the child subsequently develops an attachment to the father.

The next challenge for the child is to develop a sense of autonomy as opposed to a sense of shame and doubt. As the child begins to develop motor skills and bodily functions, parents have the opportunity to encourage mastery by focusing on progressive accomplishments as opposed to criticizing each stumble. The initial mastery begins to promote further exploration, including the seeds of sexual curiosity. Parental responsiveness to these developments in a nurturing environment leads to a sense of initiative while punitive approaches lead to a sense of child doubt. Parental patience and positive communication skills help a child develop a positive disposition towards exploring the world.

The Elementary School Years

In the ideal situation, a child accomplishes the first three life tasks and enters school with a sense of trust, a sense of autonomy and a sense of initiative. In the worst of situations, the child enters school mistrustful about the world and with feelings of shame and guilt. In the positive scenario, one hopes the school experience keeps a child moving in the positive direction. In the negative scenario the school will have a difficult time overcoming the initial negative conditions which are likely to be reinforced at home. The challenge for the parents is to ensure that children develop a sense of industry as opposed to a sense of inferiority. This responsibility involves monitoring their child's school experience and helping the child attach proper meaning to school events. One area that children have problems with is separating evaluation of their products with evaluations of their selves. When a teacher places a Gold Star, Happy Face, or *A* on an assignment, the child interprets this as "I am Good." Conversely, when a teacher places a Black Star, Sad Face, or *F* on an assignment, the child interprets the mark as "I am Bad." Parents need to help children realize that a teacher's evaluation of their work is simply that, an evaluation of whether a piece of work conformed to certain standards and expectations, without any implications regarding their self-worth.

Parents need to monitor their child's academic progress to ensure that it is commensurate with the child's abilities. If the child shows a discrepancy between the capacity to learn and what the child has actually learned, parents need to advocate that the school make every effort to determine the cause of this discrepancy. If a learning disability is documented, parents need to be actively involved in ensuring that the child has an appropriate individualized program plan in place. If the child appears to be intellectually gifted, as evidenced by quick mastery and recall of information, large vocabulary, large fund of information and focus on the principles underlying how things work, parents need to ensure that the schoolwork is appropriately challenging. Regardless of the nature of the special need, parents of children with special needs would benefit greatly through membership in organizations such as the Council for Exceptional Children, which promotes advocacy on behalf of children with special needs and provides state-of-the art information to members through journals, newsletters and conferences.

In addition to monitoring their child's academic progress, parents need to monitor their child's social development. Grusec and Lytton (1988) note the myriad ways that parents influence a child's friendships, such as choice of neighborhood, choice of school, exposure to their own friends and friends' children, supply of a homebase for interaction and active arrangement of social contacts. Since play is the vehicle for developing social competence, by involving others in interactions and rehearsals of social situations (Grusec & Lytton, 1988), parents need to ensure that their children have the opportunity to play with peers.

The Secondary School Years

The common school structure in Alberta is to have children enrolled in an elementary school from ECS-Grade 6, a junior high from Grades 7-9 and a senior high school from Grades 10-12. The transition from elementary school to junior high school requires several adjustments on the part of the student. Academically, the student is faced with several teachers at each grade level. Teachers are likely to be content experts with high expectations regarding requirements for achievement. The grading system is communicated in percentage achievement marks. Socially, the student is confronted with a larger size school that incorporates the graduating classes of several feeder schools. Although the student may have friends from the same elementary school attending the junior high school, at least 2/3 of the school will involve unfamiliar age-peers. The peer group becomes especially important during adolescence (Monks and Ferguson, 1983), particularly for adolescent females (Douvan & Adelson, 1966). Parents need to remain a source of stability in the face of a constantly changing world for the child. Parents also need the patience to deal with seemingly rebellious behavior on the part of the adolescent in attempting to exert a sense of independence. Parents also need to help their children cope with ever-increasing academic demands.

Another transition is from junior high school to high school. Once again a student finds himself or herself in a larger student body than at the previous level. High school teachers also tend to be content experts with high expectations for academic performance. In Alberta, there is a preferred course sequence that differentiates university-bound students from non-university bound students, and pressures to maintain achievement in top-tiered courses. There is a wealth of possible extra-curricular activities. One of the key developmental tasks is to develop a sense of identity that delineates one's uniqueness as a person and provides a sense of direction. During this period the adolescents will engage in interpersonal encounters called "strategic interactions" (Elkind, 1980; Goffman, 1969). Some behavioral situations that involve strategic interactions include phoning behavior, dating behavior, cutting and being cut, and concealing forbidden acts such as drinking, drug use and skipping school. Once again, parents of high school students must nurture their child's academic and social development. Parents need to work with their child in helping to plan for the child's immediate future in terms of continued educational experience or transition to the world of work. Parents need to be sensitive to the joys and pains that adolescents experience as relationships are initiated, escalated and terminated.

The University Years

The individual's transition to the university has been described earlier in this chapter and will not be repeated here. There are several challenges for parents as their children experience the university years. Parents will be faced with a financial challenge of contributing to their child's tuition, books, housing, transportation and meal expenses. Parents need to realistically determine the percentage of a child's university expenses that they are capable of providing and communicate that expectation as soon as possible. Parents will also need to cope with the psychological independence shown by their child, even in the face of financial dependence. Although the home may be a secure base from which to explore the world, the student will spend far less time with his or her parents than ever before. Parents may be confronted by changes in their child's value system as the university student is exposed to additional ways of experiencing the world. In spite of these stresses, parents need to be available to comfort their children when marks are less than expected or when relationships terminate.

The Career/Family Years

The sections on career and relationship development provided some insight regarding these perspectives from the individual's perspective. In Erikson' model, the challenge is known as generativity versus stagnation. From the parent's perspective, these transitions also present challenges. One challenge is dealing with geographic mobility. Many jobs may require the individual to move some distance from the community in which one was raised. Depending on one's chosen profession and job opportunities, this move may require a move across the country. There are fewer opportunities for personal contacts, even visits on holidays become more difficult to manage over time. So parents must balance pride in their child's accomplishment with the pain of distance. Contacts may also diminish as the individual pursues career success at the expense of familial relationships.

In terms of personal relationships, the challenge is intimacy versus isolation. At some point the individual may make the commitment for a lifelong relationship. Parents need to embrace the relationship and provide emotional support for the inevitable ups and downs that their children will face. Parents may become grandparents bonding with a new generation. Geographic distance, work involvement and family involvement may create obstacles to the relationships between adult children and their parents. As one ages this distance becomes more painful as the recognition of one's mortality becomes evident. Hopefully, the individual, when reflecting on one's life, will experience contentment with a life well-lived or, in Erickson's terms, achieve ego-integrity rather than despair.

Linking the Mazes

The scenarios presented under each section focused on typical life experiences with few extenuating circumstances. At each type of life transition, there are likely to be surprises that will complicate life even further and make transitions more difficult. During the educational transition, the individual may have parents who do not value the benefits of post-secondary education and may lack the role models of family members who have successfully negotiated the education maze. The presentation so far assumes proficiency in the language of the dominant culture yet there are increasing numbers of children in Canadian schools who have English as a second language. The educational transition for these children will be more difficult than for those proficient in English. Poverty may limit access to educational resources and may dampen aspirations as the perceived expense of higher education becomes overwhelming.

During the career transitions, technological advances may reduce the number of employees needed and necessitate retraining for those employees remaining. Even in the secure hall of academia, curriculum redesign initiatives such as moving from a course-based program to an inquiry-based one causes inner turmoil. Attractive early retirement options may lead to premature termination of a career and pressure to find satisfying income-producing work at age 55. Since retirees are often not replaced with individuals with the same level of expertise, the job demands become more difficult and frustrating for those who remain. Women may have more challenges in balancing career and family roles or adopt an interrupted career pattern to raise their children (Barocas, Reichman & Schwebel, 1983).

During the relationship transition, a joyous marriage may be terminated by a fatal car accident or a terminal illness. Cursory perusal of the obituary column in the daily newspaper provides a constant reminder of the fragility of life. A more common occurrence is dissolution of the marriage through divorce. An individual's coping with divorce parallels the bereavement process (Kressel, 1986) with stages of denial, mourning, anger and readjustment.

During the parenting transition, one may not have the luxury of delaying parenting until one's educational preparation is completed, one has negotiated the probationary career period and one is involved in a lifelong stable relationship. Families also tend to have more than one child, so the stresses of parenthood are multiplied exponentially with each child. Spouses who have experienced death or divorce might choose to remarry at some point, creating the need for the transition to remarriage and blending families.

There appear to be common challenges among life transitions. Moss and Schaefer (1986) identify these challenges as "adaptive tasks" that are necessary for coping with life transitions. The first set of tasks involves establishing the meaning and personal significance of the situation. The second set of tasks involves confronting reality and responding to the requirements of the external situation. The third set of tasks involves sustaining relationships with family, friends and other individuals who might be helpful. The fourth set of tasks involves managing upsetting feelings to maintain emotional balance. The final set of tasks involves preserving a satisfactory sense of self and sense of competence. Moos and Schaefer (1986) suggest that three broad types of coping skills can enhance one's effectiveness in coping with transitions: appraisal-focused coping, problem-focused coping and emotion-focused coping. In appraisal-focused coping, the individual focuses on a logical analysis of the situation, recollection of past successes in dealing with problems and mental rehearsal of coping with problem situations. In problem-focused coping the individual seeks information and support and applies problem-solving strategies. In emotion-focused coping, the individual vacillates between affective regulation and emotional discharge, eventually developing resigned acceptance. Effective use of these skills provides the cognitive, affective and behavioral resources for coping with life transitions.

References

Ainsworth. M. D. S. (1964). "Patterns of attachment behavior shown by the infant in interaction with his mother." *Merrill-Palmer Quarterly, 10*, 51-58.

Ainsworth, M. D. S., Bell, S. M. & Stayton, D. J. (1974). "Infant-mother attachment and social development: 'Socialization' as a product of reciprocal responsiveness to signals." In M. P. M. Richards (Ed.), *The integration of a child into a social world* (pp. 99-135). London: Cambridge University Press.

Altman, I. & Taylor, D. A. (1973). *Social penetration: The development of interpersonal relationships.* New York: Holt, Rinehart & Winston.

Barocas, H., Reichman, W. & Schwebel, A. J. (1983). *Personal adjustment and growth: A life-span approach.* New York: St Martin's Press.

Bowlby, J. (1971). *Attachment and loss: Attachment* (Vol. I). London: Pelican Books.

Bransky, T., Jenkins-Friedman, R. & Murphy, D. (1987). "Identifying and working with gifted students 'at risk' for disabling perfectionism." In *Research Briefs 1987* (pp. 14-16). Circle Pines, MN: National Association for Gifted Children.

Branden, N. (1988). "A vision of romantic love." In R. J. Sternberg & M. L. Barnes (Eds.), *The psychology of love* (pp. 218-231). New Haven: Yale University Press.

Douvan, E. & Adelson, J. (1966). *The adolescent experience.* New York: Wiley.

Elkind, D. (1980). "Strategic interactions." In J. Adelson (Ed.), *Handbook of adolescent development* (pp. 432-444). New York: Wiley.

Erikson, E. (1951). *Childhood and society.* New York: Norton.

Friedman, P. G. (1978, November). *Social giftedness: Description and development.* Paper presented at the meeting of the National Association for Gifted Children, Houston.

Grusec, J. E. & Lytton, H. (1988). *Social development: History, theory, and research.* New York: Springer-Verlag.

Hatfield, E. (1988). "Passionate and companionate love." In R. J. Sternberg & M. L. Barnes (Eds.), *The psychology of love* (pp. 191-217). New Haven: Yale University Press.

Hollingshead, A. B. & Redlich, F. C. (1958). *Social class and mental illness.* New York: Wiley.

Jourard, S. M. (1971). *Self-disclosure: An experimental analysis of the transparent self.* New York: Wiley.

Kressel, K. (1986). "Patterns of coping in divorce." In R. H. Moos (Ed.), *Coping with life crises* (pp. 145-153). New York: Plenum.

Leibowitz, M. R. (1983). *The chemistry of love.* Boston: Little, Brown.

Monks, F. J. & Ferguson, T. J. (1983). "Gifted adolescents: An analysis of their psychosocial development." *Journal of Youth and Adolescence, 12,* 1-18.

Moos, R. H. & Schaefer, J. A. (1986). "Life transitions and crises: A conceptual overview." In R. H. Moos (Ed.), *Coping with life crises* (pp. 3-28). New York: Plenum.

Sternberg, R. J. (1986). "A triangular theory of love." *Psychological Review, 93,* 119-135.

Sternberg, R. J. (1988). "Triangulating love." In R. J. Sternberg & M. L. Barnes (Ed.), *The psychology of love* (pp. 119-138). New Haven: Yale University press.

Sternberg, R. J. & Barnes, M. L. (1985). "Real and ideal others in romantic relationships: Is four a crowd?" *Journal of Personality and Social Psychology, 49,* 1589-1596.

Wallerstein, J. S. (1986). "Children of divorce: The psychological tasks of the child." In R. H. Moos (Ed.), *Coping with life crises* (pp. 35-48). New York: Plenum.

Wiemann, J. M. (1977). "Explication and test of a model of communication competence." *Human Communication Research, 3,* 195-213.

Chapter 7
Navigating Transitions Well: Success Stories

*E. Lisbeth Donaldson, Bryan Hiebert,
Michael Pyryt, Nancy Arthur*

Introduction

The four stories narrated in this chapter represent the transitions that have been discussed more generically in previous chapters. They personalize social trends and psychological developments but names and some details have been changed to ensure anonymity. Perhaps some aspect of these journeys will be similar to that of a reader. Everyone has a story about transitions in their lives, however, not everyone shares the wisdom that evolves from the experiences. Personal pain and shame may contribute to silencing; some think their story might not have value to other people. Also, some individuals don't stop to reflect upon a transition, thus maximizing the opportunity to learn. This chapter is an encouragement to voice successes enjoyed during important life transitions and to discuss associated tensions so they might be reduced. It is an opportunity for readers to become part of this book.

May: A geographer and feminist who is doing well but . . .

E. Lisbeth Donaldson

May graduated from the University of Calgary with a geography degree in 1995 and is now an environmental analyst for a large corporation. She describes herself as "very independent. I like to do my own thing." She described her transition from high school as easy, noting that high school classes were smaller; there were closer relationships with teachers. May attended first-year university orientation and thought it "reduced shock" as she knew the buildings. She traveled by C-train to campus five days per week, usually staying from 9 a.m. to 5 p.m. and bringing her lunch. "Marks suffered" after arrival at university, although she studied approximately 20 hours per week, more at exam time. It took six years to complete the degree and she dropped courses during first year; calculus was a problem. She thought that some subjects, especially math, were poorly linked in content between high school and university. Organic chemistry, a component of the first-year chemistry course, is valuable knowledge in her work. English has always been a strong subject but she preferred science, noting the growth in environmental employment opportunities. The best part of attending university were the final two years because she liked the focus of her classes very much: they were smaller and people with similar interests "could connect"; the worst part was a music history course in first year in which she was the only non-major. Her favorite haunts on campus were Earth Sciences, Mac Hall, the gym and library. She often used the gym and ran in the Oval but she belonged only to the biosciences social group.

Although she received an A on the Grade 12 departmental biology exam, her teacher told her she'd "never make it in science." At university, however, she thought there were few problems, less than with older male high school teachers. She didn't join the campus Women in Science and Engineering (WISE) group, but now is part of a women in the workforce group, stating that age and gender discrimination are "blatant." When asked if women make a difference in science, she stated that women in scientific fields are very rare, especially younger women. May describes her family (of two younger sisters, one of whom "might" eventually attend college, and mother) as "math illiterate," excepting her father. Three years ago she moved from the family home and lives downtown where she walks to work.

Tuition "tripled" during the undergraduate period but she has no debts. She worked full-time during the summers while at university but didn't work during the term. The work was in the environmental department at the same company where she is now employed. At that time her father, an engineer, was working there and as a student she approached the manager of the environmental department. Her current employment is full-time contract work so benefits are limited, but the salary approximates $3000 per month; when the hiring freeze ends she expects to become a permanent employee. She likes her work as coordinator of a program on climate change for Canada but hopes in five years to be an international consultant, preferably in South America. She's taking Spanish and thinks she'll eventually do a Masters.

May doesn't make friends easily but maintains friendships well, saying she has about 10 close friends. Some high school classmates are married with children and they appear to enjoy their different life paths. She stated that few students from her high school wanted to attend university. She doesn't plan to marry but hopes to travel and plans a two week research assistantship at Amazonia University in Brazil as part of her summer vacation.

May noted that science is closely "tied in with business" and that affects the economy and social system, particularly in a capitalist society. She defines science as a "search for knowledge, hopefully objective and understanding the links." One reason for selecting geography was that it didn't "cut off" the social aspect of science. She thinks that science makes a positive impact but notes there's "a lot of negative stuff going on out there." She noted that the rain forest action group has many men in it. "Personally I'm a tree hugger but not an enviro-nazi." Asked about Canadian achievements, she mentioned meeting David Suzuki recently and was impressed with his Foundation; also several chemists in her company are doing "important work" in health care.

Some of her university friends have not found "proper work in their field" and "that's really disappointing – I hate to see that."

This young woman is a good example of a student who had an easy passage during the transition from high school to university and from university to work, yet during her undergraduate years she had a period during which she floundered. Time-to-completion of her undergraduate degree was extended when she did poorly in mathematics, a pre-requisite for the science program. Although she had good study habits and self discipline, it took six years to graduate. Her interest in sports is one of the distinguishing markers of women who do well in a traditional career.

She is typical of the many women who prefer the human aspect of science. As the talent pool of women scientists and engineers has increased, they tend to select fields in which "the life force" is predominant, such as ecology. Although she resisted the negative messages of high school teachers, when gender constraints were less obvious, she did not seek support at university to explore career opportunities; now, she is an active feminist interested in more workplace equity. She has done well but it is possible that she is an underachiever with respect to her undergraduate path and will undoubtedly select her Masters program with more awareness. Although she says she doesn't plan to marry, she already demonstrates many aspects of a female career path which is more plateaued, less hierarchical. The eldest of three daughters whose father is an engineer, she may well be more career oriented than her two sisters.

As a student, May used family connections, obtaining relevant part-time work that positioned her very well for career-level employment. At the time of graduation, she had a network of workplace contacts and relevant employment experience. Job entry with full-time contract work is a common stepping stone for many university graduates but she may not obtain permanent employment as quickly as an engineer or hard scientist. Nevertheless, she should have an interesting career and a fulfilling life. But it will be decades before women such as May receive an education that encourages maximum development of their unique talents.

Coming to Canada: A Transition Through Immigration

Nancy Arthur

Tamara is a woman in her 20s who voluntarily immigrated to Canada two years ago. In the former Communist regime of her country of origin, she struggled with concerns about issues of safety, economic stability and restrictions of personal freedom. Her decision to immigrate was prompted by dissonance about what she believed was possible to create and what her local situation could offer. Her keen interest in contributing to society was being stifled by lack of opportunities for social change. Since arriving in Canada two years ago, increasing levels of political conflict and violence in her country of origin have validated her decision.

The early transition to Canada was associated with both emotional and physical symptoms of stress. As an independent immigrant, Tamara's residency was conditional upon self-sufficiency. She was determined to prove her independence. Along with this drive, she felt immediate pressure to secure employment while simultaneously learning about local structures and systems. Initial employment experiences prompted the difficult realization that her credentials would not be transferable to the Canadian labor market. After six years of university education and two professional degrees in medicine and social work, Tamara faced limited options.

> What made me more frustrated was that I would go and apply and people would say, "Oh, you are very highly qualified; Oh, you will get a job", and then the answer was, "Unfortunately we cannot give it to you because you don't have Canadian experience." So then I started questioning what this Canadian experience is all about. I'm sure that has to do with certain ways that people work here in Canada, but to me,

at the same time, people were putting too much emphasis on a kind of idealistic concept.

Tamara had to manage the transition to a new country by herself. She remembers renting her first apartment in which she sat with no familiar possessions and nobody to talk to. Previously, she had a job that was respected and that afforded her material comforts in daily living. She missed being part of a family and being well known in the local community. Social status changes for her were less about material possessions than longing for a sense of belonging.

I had my status, which made me equal to everybody that I met. I come to Canada ... first of all I don't have status at all, but in addition to that is that you are not accepted as well, I mean you are rejected instead. So, it was really hard.

Tamara's early transition to life in Canada was characterized by the absence of social support and personal validation. She felt isolated without family and friends to share experiences.

Now, when I go back to my memories I feel that I would have done much better in handling this stress, if I had people around me. I remember that I was quite lonely, absolutely lonely in every sense.

She missed her long-standing relationships and noticed differences in the social interactions of the local community. New relationships in Canada lacked the intimacy of family and friends.

People have quite a private life in Canada. In terms of the culture, it is quite different from back home in my country. I mean, business is business, a little bit of a social life, and that's it.

How has this immigrant woman coped with her cross-cultural transition? Tamara identified her knowledge and experience prior to departing for Canada as a general preparation for coping. Traveling to other foreign countries in Europe gave her some cross-cultural experience and helped prepare her for new cultural contrasts. While language acquisition continues to be an ongoing learning process, English language skills allowed her to communicate needs and research local resources. Contact with immigrant-serving agencies for transition assistance was discouraging, initially, as only general services were available. Eventually, formal assistance offered by the Calgary Catholic Immigration Society that was tailored to her current needs for employment became a valuable coping resource. Tamara was clear about what the direction she was taking; she needed someone to help her link with local opportunities.

At the end what was helpful, was finding somebody ... a resettlement counselor who read me differently from other clients that he was serving.

Tamara' sense of self-direction and positive attitude for learning about Canadian culture are ways of coping that are connected to her personal goals for success. Her resilience in adversity is strongly connected to building a future for herself and for her family.

> I would say simply, being clear about where do you want to go. That's the major coping skill that I see for myself. That's where I find my coping on whatever I face, kind of analyzing where I am and then finding out where I want to go from here.

Her measure of personal success in cross-cultural transition is based upon her progress towards reaching short- and long-term goals. Despite the frustrations associated with a new cultural context, she transcends adversity through commitment to goals for living in Canada.

Stable employment connected to her professional expertise has eased many transition concerns. Tamara also copes through social comparison of her own situation to the circumstances of immigrant and refugee groups with whom she works. Coping is also enhanced through recognizing the contributions that she is making to others during settlement into the local community.

After living in Canada for 15 months, Tamara decided to return home to reconnect with her family and friends. She was not prepared for the degree of change she would face in her home country. Longing for connection with her family and friends, she was startled by what she saw.

> When I went there, I was quite shocked really, I mean seeing now in reality what people have described, the fact that it wasn't any longer the country with prosperity as I left the country when I came here. I believe those were circumstances that had made people migrate. When I went there I didn't find a lot of people that I was expecting to meet, I mean my old friends.

Tamara felt distressed about the condition of her country and a sense of alienation from the home that she had longed to visit.

> My country is no longer any place where you can return so this was the hurting part of, hearing or finding out that a lot of your friends have left the country. . . . Because I didn't find any longer my friends I use to walk with in the street or in public places, and not seeing any longer the faces that I knew . . . for me it made me feel than I'm a stranger as well . . . it's not as comforting as it was.

Experiencing these changes in her country brought a surprising discovery about her cross-cultural adjustment in Canada. She realized how much she had personally changed.

> On my way back to Canada, this was instinctively, I mean it's not that I gave thought to it or whatever, but on my way to Canada finding

things in order ... quite settled in every sense ... at the airport, it made me feel oh my gosh I feel so relieved and relaxed to be in Canada, to be back ... I mean, okay, then I have done quite a bit in those months ... makes you much more clear ...

Experiencing the changes in her home country helped Tamara to acknowledge the positive changes that she associates with her life in Canada and has helped to gain perspective about her country of origin. Rather than drawing comparisons based upon what she was missing from her former home, she is able to consider the gains that she has made in her new life in Canada.

Tamara has identified future challenges for managing her cross-cultural transition. Satisfying employment gives her a basis from which to pursue other areas of adjustment. In the area of social support, Tamara acknowledges the difference that making friends has for her life in Canada. She feels more comfortable knowing that if she needed someone she has people in the local community that she can contact. However, she continues to miss the intimate connection of family. "I miss what is unreplaceable, I think, which is the family." Tamara is currently directing her efforts towards sponsorship for two of her family members to immigrate to Canada. The goal of reuniting with family in Canada is a source of motivation in her current cultural context. If she is successful in this endeavor, her fiancé will join her and they will build a life in Canada as a couple.

Another future transition need is her commitment to pursue Canadian professional credentials.

It is hard ... because, in the meantime that I'm thinking about my career, I'm thinking about my family so, to handle them both is quite difficult ... right, it's a matter of energy and time but, I ask myself to do so, I really have to, but when I don't know yet ...

Juggling both financial responsibilities to support herself and her family and finding ways to improve her professional qualifications is viewed as a major challenge. Another challenge identified for the future process of transition is reconciling her original cultural values and ways of operating in new cultural contexts. Despite the need to demonstrate competence in new cultural ways, Tamara believes that it is also important to maintain her cultural identity.

It's a dilemma because, in order to be accepted more and more you kind of have to develop other skills that make you Canadian, but on the other hand those things are inside me ... I think I would elaborate a little bit more in terms of accepting or keeping my own ones as well as the Canadian way.

Although Tamara feels that she has expended considerable effort to learn about and practise new forms of cultured behavior, she is attempting to maintain her original cultural identity and find avenues for fuller self-expression. Otherwise, she believes she will continue to feel restricted and a lack of validation for her contribution to roles and relationships in Canadian society. Managing her cross-cultural transition in the future requires finding avenues to maintain her original culture while practicing new ways of living in Canada. Tamara believes that there are many advantages to living with a bi-cultural identity. While continuing to learn about Canadian practices, she looks forward to working in ways that show the strengths of her own cultural background. The experiences of this immigrant woman reminds us that successful cross-cultural transitions entail moving from a monocultural view to multicultured perspectives of the world. Ultimately, it is hoped that for Tamara and other immigrants, the people with whom they interact will become as open to learning about their culture as they have been to learning about life in Canada.

The Case of David:
From Discovery Through Educational Development

Michael C. Pyryt

David represents the story of numerous youth who have successfully participated in the Study of Mathematically Precocious Youth (SMPY), which was briefly described in Chapter 5. The story focuses on the transition from initial discovery in Grade 7 through graduate school.

Although David grew up in the United States, his story is relevant to the Canadian context. Recently a 10-year-old student in Calgary scored a 710 (top 2%) on the mathematics portion of the Scholastic Aptitude Test. Currently, it is possible for seventh graders in Canada to participate in a Talent Search at the University of Toronto conducted in collaboration with Duke University that is very similar to the contest that David participated in. In the near future, Canadian students might participate in a Canada-wide talent search at the University of Calgary.

During Fall term of his Grade 7 year, David received a note from his school counsellor that he was eligible to participate in the upcoming Talent Search conducted by the Study of Mathematically Precocious Youth at The Johns Hopkins University. To be eligible for the contest one needed to be a seventh grader who scored in the top 3 percent on a standardized test in either mathematics, language arts or overall achievement composite in the most recent testing. David became eligible by scoring at the 98th percentile on the mathematics section of the Comprehensive Test of Basic Skills taken in Grade 6. The contest consists of taking the *Scholastic Aptitude Tests* (SAT), which are typically given to students in Grade 11 and Grade 12 aspiring to enter universities in the United States. The mathematics section consists primarily of algebra, geometry and trigonometry. The verbal section consists primarily of vocabulary and reading comprehension. The Test of Standard Written English consists of the mechanical skills of writing. Since David never formally had a course in algebra, geometry or trigonometry, he wondered whether the test would be too difficult for him. David had been exposed to these concepts by studing some of the mathematics books available in the home, doing mathematics puzzles and playing mathematical computer games. His parents (father an engineer and mother an economist) convinced David that he should participate in the contest for the potential educational benefits that might accrue and were happy to write a cheque for the $60.00 U.S. that participation in the contest would cost. Upon entering the contest in October, David received from the Educational Testing Service a practice booklet and a copy of an old test as a sample. David studied the practice booklet and sample test and participated in the Talent Search in January.

In March, David received the news. His scores on the SAT placed him in the 90th, 84th and 90th percentiles for university bound high school seniors on the mathematics, verbal and written English sections of the SAT respectively. On the advice of personnel from Johns Hopkins, David was given the *Differential Aptitude Tests – Level I*, a multi-aptitude battery meant for high school students, the *Standard and Advanced Progressive Matrices*, measures of non-verbal reasoning ability, the *Strong Interest Inventory*, a personality measure of career interests, and the *Allport-Vernon-Lindzey Study Of Values*, a measure that provides an intra-individual profile of value preferences. David's performance on the *Differential Aptitude Tests* indicated superior abilities in abstract reasoning, mechanical reasoning and space relations, in addition to superior numerical ability and verbal reasoning. David's non-verbal reasoning ability on the *Advanced Progressive Matrices* indicated he functioned similar to university-level students. His scores on the *Strong Interest Inventory* indicated that his rsponses were most similar to individuals in Investigative type occupations. David's profile on the *Allport-Vernon-Lindzey Study of Values* indicated that David was most interested in discovering truth, given his high score on the Theoretical scale, and least interested in power, given his low score on the Political scale. This information was used to develop an educational plan for David.

In Grade 8, David completed all of the core subjects for both Grades 8 and 9 through a technique called Diagnostic Testing – Prescriptive Instruction (DT-PI). In this technique, a comprehensive Final examination, either as a standardized or teacher-made test, is given as a pretest. The test performance is analyzed in terms of the concepts covered by each item. Students are assumed to know a concept if they can answer correctly those items that reflect the concept. Students are only taught the concepts covered by the items a student gets wrong. When the students show mastery of these concepts through homework, quizzes and tests, they are given a parallel form (same concepts, different items) of the comprehensive final examination. When they meet a specified cut-off, they begin to study the next subject. Through this technique, David also mastered the required curriculum in Algebra I, Plane Geometry, Algebra II and Analytical Geometry.

David entered Universal High, a comprehensive public high school, at age 14. The plan was for David to have a rewarding intellectual and social experience. David took Trigonometry in Grade 10, Calculus in Grade 11 and Advanced Placement Calculus in Grade 12. For Foreign Language, David studied Latin, French and German. His Language Arts curriculum also included an Advanced Placement English Course. In the sciences, David took Biology, Chemistry, Physics and Advanced Placement Biology. David also took courses in History, Geography and Psychology. After taking the Advanced Placement courses, David took the Advanced Placement Tests administered by the Educational Testing Service. The test are scored on a "1" to "5" scale. Students earning a "4" or a "5" are typically awarded the equivalent of a year's worth of subject matter credit at a university. (Some universities award credit for a score of "3"). David earned a "5" on both Advanced Placement Calculus and Advanced Placement Biology and a "4" on Advanced Placement English. In addition to his Advanced Placement performance, David enroled in an Astronomy course and a Computer Science course at a nearby university during the summers following his Grade 10 and Grade 11 years and earned an "A" in both courses. In the March of his Grade 11 year, David retook the *Scholastic Aptitude Tests* and scored in the 99.9th, the 98th and the 98th on the mathematics, verbal and written English sections of the SATs respectively. During his high school years David participated in the Debating Society, the Yearbook Committee and the Cross-Country Team. He had a few close friends and many acquaintances. In November of his Grade 12 year, David applied as an Early Admission candidate to The Johns Hopkins University and received notice of his acceptance and financial aid package, which consisted of scholarship, student loan guarantees and opportunities for work-study arrangements in February.

David enroled at Johns Hopkins at age 17 as a Biology major. Through his success on the three Advanced Placement Tests and two university courses taken while in high school, David entered Johns Hopkins with 32 of the required 120 credits accumulated. The Advanced Placement credits also permitted David to take advanced courses a year earlier than normal. Instead of taking General Biology his first year, for example, David took Cell Biology and Biochemistry. In his second year, David took Biophysics. At the end of his second year, David applied for and was admitted to the B.Sc./M.Sc program in Biology. This competitive program makes it possible to earn Bachelor of Science and Master of Science degrees simultaneously in four years. In his third and fourth years of university, David worked in a professor's laboratory under the supervision of post-doctoral students, took graduate level biology courses, and conducted independent research on "gene mapping." He also completed the distribution requirements for his Bachelor of Science Degree, which for David included additional coursework in French, Literature, Social Sciences and Quantitative Studies. David fit in well with the other students at Johns Hopkins (80% of whom aspire to a post-baccalaureate degree), who generally are intelligent, conscientious and achievement-oriented. Each spring, David (like all Hopkins students, faculty and alumni) lived and died with the successes and disappointments of the lacrosse team, which perennially competed for the National Championship in Field Lacrosse. He had a few intimate relationships which were the source of great joy and great pain. He graduated from Johns Hopkins at age of 21 years with both a Bachelor of Science and a Master of Science degree completing a thesis on *"Gene Profiles of Diabetic and Non-Diabetic Drosophilia."* His overall GPA of 3.92 earned David Departmental Honours in Biology and election into Phi Beta Kappa.

Upon the advice and with a strong letter of recommendation from Dr. McNally, his thesis adviser, David applied to and was accepted at the California Institute of Technology participating in the human genome project coordinated by Dr. Pinot, a Nobel Laureate. He received a three-year Graduate Fellowship from the National Science Foundation. David is in the process of completing his dissertation and entertaining post-doctoral offers at The University of Chicago and Stanford.

Pierre:
From Social Assistance to Meaningful Employment

Bryan Hiebert

Background

Pierre Lagrande was from a medium sized town in Atlantic Canada. His mother was English and his father was French. He lived in an English neighborhood of what was predominately a francophone community. His parents were on welfare and his grandparents were as well. His father and mother both worked periodically for some extra "under-the-table" money, but there never seemed to be enough money to go around. Pierre was a short person, poorly dressed and with a name like "Lagrande" he received a lot of teasing about the mismatch between his name and his stature.

Pierre did not like school and seldom read anything except comic books. His parents did not spend much time reading either and in fact they never subscribed to the newspaper, adopting the attitude that it was a waste of money to buy a newspaper when it was all on television anyway. Given this context, it is not surprising that Pierre did not do well in school: he had no friends, the other students teased him and the teachers always seemed to be on his back. School was not a nice place to be, but there did not seem to be any better places, so he stuck it out.

The Tide Turns

In grade 11, Pierre was persuaded to participate in an experimental career education program in his school. He thought it would be better than his regular school subject and so agreed to participate. What he received was very different than what he expected.

The experimental program was aimed at developing an internal locus of control regarding one's career. The program began by asking people to look inside themselves, in order to discover what sorts of things they liked to do and why they liked to do those things. It then went on to help the young people identify the skills within those tasks that could be marketed to obtain employment. The program then shifted to an exploration of the kinds of things that they were good at. These were combined with the skills resulting from enjoyable activities to form a master list of the skills and personal qualities that they could use to market themselves to a future employer.

The next phase in the experimental program was to look at the whole issue of self-esteem. Pierre had never given it much thought. He "knew" that he was no good at school and that there were few other things he was any good at. He had heard his teachers lamenting about how he was not working up to potential, but he did not know what to do about it. Part of the program had participants spend at least 1 hour each day doing something that they really truly liked. They also kept track of the things they were saying to themselves, and tried to focus more on saying things to themselves that were more realistic and focused more on their accomplishments. Through this process a fundamental change began to take place. School was still a drag and he could hardly wait to be out. BUT, he did not mind it as much as before, and it seemed to him like his marks were improving as well.

The last aspect of the program was to look at potential occupations that the students might be interested in and which they might be able market to a potential employer. Students became more aware of the fact that even in their community, where it seemed like there were few options, employers were still hiring people and other students like him were finding part-time work. Some even found jobs that were paying enough money to allow them to leave school and find their own place to live. For the first time in as far back as he could remember, Pierre actually felt proud of himself. In fact when the evaluation of the experimental program was being done, he told the expert from the local university that while participating in this program it was "the first time in my life that I have felt proud of myself."

Today, Pierre is employed as a sales clerk in a large hardware chain. By some people's standards, it is a mediocre job. However, for Pierre it continues to be very fulfilling. He likes meeting people and he especially feels good when they thank him for assisting them. His manager reports that he has a cheerful attitude, is a good team player and is a dependable member of the department team. Pierre lives in a basement suite, sharing rent with a friend he met at the hardware store. The rest of his family still lives on welfare. Pierre does not criticize them for that, but he is quite happy that he has a regular job with reasonable pay. He spends a lot of time with his room mate and recently has started attending evening classes in folk music. He's learning to play the guitar. He knows that his friends and his other social activities help him to keep focused on his own personal goals and not get drawn back into his old habits. The fact that Pierre is the first person in three generations of his family to get off welfare not only was good for the field test of the new program, but it was also a very positive experience for Pierre.

As a finale, you are invited to share your story about a successful transitional milestone.

Chapter 8
Forecasting: Millennia Transition Trends

*Nancy Arthur, Bryan Hiebert,
E.L. Donaldson, Michael Pyryt*

As *Making Transitions Work* is published, the world is preparing for the transition of a century ending and a new one beginning. The year 2000 also introduces a new millenium, provoking a larger vision of a thousand years of change. It appears timely to reflect on the transitions that have occurred in the last century and consider their influence for emerging challenges that Canadians will face. What can we learn from the transitions of this century that will assist people to prepare for their lives in the 21st century? If the past is the best predictor of the future, there are two trends that are ensured: 1) rapid change will be an integral part of life beyond the year 2000, and 2) people will need to cope with immense pressures during ongoing life transitions. The authors of this book considered two themes they believe fundamental to people's lives in the future. The topics that they chose to discuss include the transition to a global marketplace, listening to the voices of youth, 25 years in the marketplace, the economics of higher education and impact of technology, and preparing for future change.

The Transition to the Global Marketplace

Without question, the future of Canada's economy is inextricably defined by our capacity to be competitive in the international marketplace through interdependent relations with other countries. Increasing access to global markets is already changing the ways in which Canadians approach education and employment. Although Canada's emerging role in international trade is essential for the economic viability of our nation, it is timely to consider how this direction of future progress may impact the lives of individuals. The global economy has implications on many levels including the career development of individuals, family relations and Canada's role in international development.

With increasing expectations that employees take on an international role in either local settings and in settings of other countries, Canadians must be prepared for careers that involve working with people from other nations. Currently, most adults are exposed to international work on the basis of their professional expertise for a particular project. This "ad hoc" entrance into the international arena leaves many employees ill-prepared for the demands of working in unfamiliar cultural contexts. While organizations are beginning to attend to the preparation of employees for cross-cultural work transitions, training is typically implemented for specific work projects. The increasing salience of the global economy demands that we rethink our approach to preparing a workforce that is skilled not only in designated areas of technical expertise but also in their preparation for working in the international marketplace. Rather than viewing international roles as an exception in adult careers, the changing world of work in the millenium requires that international work be viewed as an integral aspect of career development. In order to equip youth for the workplace of the future, career planning must include preparation for working with people from other countries. Second language fluency, knowledge of socio-political and economic systems, education abroad, travel experience, knowledge of cultural differences, and skills for managing cross-cultural transitions are key areas to integrate into career planning for the global economy of the new millenium. Those people who have had the foresight to incorporate cross-cultural competencies into their career development will have a tremendous advantage in the workplace of the future.

The increased access to international markets will also create additional opportunities for worker mobility. As migrant workers from diverse cultural backgrounds move between the borders of international business and education, the need to prepare individuals for working and learning in cross-cultural environments must be underscored. Success in new cultural environments depends upon the degree to which people can navigate the demands of new norms for behavior and the local systems of the community. Although there is growing recognition of the need to prepare individual workers and students for cross cultural transition, less attention has been paid to the impact of worker mobility on family members. The opportunity to work or study in another country often requires family members to make hard decisions about the implications for family functioning. One member of the family may be required to be away from the family unit for an extended period of time.

Alternatively, work assignments may be designed for intensive work activities and return visits home. This can lead to considerable disruption to families in terms of shifting role responsibilites and the need to reorganize with the flow of work assignments. Families may also have to make decisions about whether to relocate to another country on a temporary or extended basis. While there are usually economic benefits associated with international work assignments, the impacts of separation and loss of usual social supports during these transitions have not been adequately addressed in terms of the effects on family relationships and long-term functioning. While organizations move to prepare workers for entering into international roles, families will also require assistance to prepare for the impact of increasing demands for mobility.

Canada's increasing access to the global economy in the new millenium undoubtedly poses many new opportunities for employment and education in other countries. Along with these opportunities comes the need to prepare individuals and families to effectively manage the accompanying transitions. Apart from the implications for career development, Canada's involvement in the global marketplace must also be considered from the viewpoint of international development. While the motives directing international partnerships are inextricably bound to economic growth and financial gains, corresponding attention needs to be paid to the ethical implications of Canada's role in the international marketplace. Is it reasonable for Canada to be trade partners with any country so long as economic growth is ensured? With what countries will Canada promote the exchange of international students and foreign expertise? To what countries will we choose to export our natural resources and transfer of technology? What leverage can Canada have through trade partnerships to impact local conditions in countries with poor records of human rights violations? Underpinning these questions are values which are often in conflict regarding Canada's influence to impact the power basis of both developed and non-developed countries. As the Canadian private sector, educational institutions and levels of government seize opportunities for expanded markets, there are critical question to be addressed concerning Canada's role in relationships with other nations.

Listening to the Voices of Youth

Numerous studies have indicated that there are dramatic differences in the perceptions held by adults and students about the needs of youth today. For the most part, adults tend to be problem oriented, commenting on the difficulties that young people face and on the hassles that occur between young people and adults. The common perception of adults seems tied to the myth that adolescence is of necessity a time of turbulence. Evidence we have cited in this book challenges that common misperception and suggests that when young people strike out, it is a result of a sense of frustration about their lack of skill at dealing with troublesome situations. Many studies have indicated that young people want to identify solutions to the problems they encounter. They want to learn skills for dealing more effectively with the demands they face. Young people want better skills for dealing with the multitude of interpersonal situations in which they are involved. They often are relatively happy with their interactions with peers, but would like better skills for dealing with the adults with whom they interact. Young people see career planning as very important and want better skills for handling the transition from schooling to gainful employment. They want to be better able to manage the stress they experience, and they see a need to be better at building their self-esteem. If adults were more willing to listen to the voices of young people, they would be in a better position to foster experiences that help prepare youth for the world of today, rather than dwelling on an approach that likely is outdated.

In many parts of our country, there is a growing movement to "return to the basics." However, this movement appears to be misguided. Invariably, the "basics" to which we are being encouraged to return are a variation on the "3 Rs," reading, writing, and arithmetic. These were the core subjects in school through the middle half of the current century. They were necessary skills to succeed in life. However, society has changed dramatically over the past 20 years, and the "basic" skills necessary to become a functioning member of society are quite different today than they were two decades ago. The skills needed for survival today more likely involve the set of employability skills outlined by the Conference Board of Canada (1992). These involve basic literacy and higher order thinking skills, personal management skills and team work skills. To return to the basics of half a century ago is to do a disservice to the youth of today. Young people recognize that more contemporary skills are needed. If adults were better at listening to the voices of youth, they would be better able to understand what is needed to be successful in the world of today.

A grade 11 student summarizes the situation best. We had been debriefing a focus group in the needs assessment study described in Chapter 3. Her comment was that this was the first time in her school experience that anyone had ever asked for her input on what she thought she needed to learn and actually listened to what she had to say. It's a sad indictment on our current top-heavy way of approaching young people. We would encourage adults to focus more attention on rectifying the situation.

Lighten Up on Youth

A second message to parents and teachers would be to lighten up on the pressure. As David Elkind pointed out several years ago (Elkind, 1988), humans typically live about 60-70 years of their lives as adults. What is the hurry to end childhood? Much of the pressure young people experience is aimed at forcing them into adult roles, often without adequate preparation. When children "graduate" from kindergarten with cap and gown, what is left to be special when they finish high school or university? For many children, much of their childhood lost to premature exposure to adult roles and pressure to enter an adult rat race that does not even make sense to adults, let alone to children.

Youth is a time for exploring, yet many young people are discouraged from exploration. Well-meaning adults continue to pressure young people to decide on an occupational destination in the misguided belief that it is important to decide on an occupation early. These adults seem to forget that they themselves have changed occupations four or five times in their careers, and that was at a time then the labor force was more stable and jobs were plentiful. The "High 5 (+1)" (Day, Redekopp & Robb, 1994; Redekopp, Day & Robb, 1995) needs to be a more apparent message. Exploration and creation of multiple alternatives need to be more central messages. Focusing on process and being less concerned about outcome needs to become more common. The second part of our message to adults would be to let up on the pressure and encourage your sons and daughters to explore their options, clarify their values and set a personal vision for their lives. Then provide emotional support to pursue their dreams and discover their passions in life.

Young people today face a different world with different challenges than their parents faced. To successfully navigate the transitions they will encounter, they need different skill sets than those that were used by their parents. For the most part, young people are aware of the changed context and are identifying the skills they need to be successful. They sometimes need help clarifying direction or accessing the resources they require. A partnership approach where youth and adults are working together to identify areas of need and develop programs and resources to address those needs is likely to be less fraught with hassles and more successful in preparing young people for the multitude of transitions they will experience.

25 years in the Marketplace: Who needs more?

The retirement stereotype of the faithful employee receiving a handshake and a gold watch after 25 years of service is a dated image from the last century: we have been warned that the future involves multiple serial careers, some of which have not yet been imagined. Nevertheless, will it be necessary to work more than 25 years? Among the dynamics of the current marketplace chaos, some trends are becoming more clear and it is possible to chart an adult career path that places the employment aspect of a life cycle into perspective. Demographics, economics, finances, personal identity and societal mores are all important components. No one, of course, can avoid the fallout from a major disaster such as large scale war, disruptive weather events, or disease, but assuming normal ranges and diversity within a Western life cycle, adult men and women can anticipate living longer but needing to work less.

The first question to ask is perhaps which 25 years? Given that more education is required of more people, youth are staying in school longer. However, if a young person enters the adult labor market at age 25 and remains appropriately employed for a quarter of a century, most basic needs will have been met. Even if the person has career stopout time for further education and children, income-producing years need not total more than 25 years although the chronological period may be elongated. The higher the level of education, the higher the income, therefore people with fewer qualifications may work longer. A phase in and phase out period of part-time work might be the model some individuals prefer. But the economic reasons for working more than 25 years seem to be less persuasive than those related to self-identity.

For many people, work is a symbol of self-esteem and status: it is how a person indicates he or she is useful, a contributing citizen of society. It is a home away from home in which colleagues become closer than some family or neighbors; important passages such as birthdays, weddings, funerals are observed with regularity, providing attention that some adults would receive privately. When asked, "what do you do?", people reply with descriptions about their employment role. It is the question women who are "housewives" and "stay at home mums" learn to dread. But, 7 of 10 adult women are now working at paid employment outside the home and many of those at home are not planning to remain there for 25 years of their adult life. Men have especially been socialized into work-related identities because of perceptions about being the family "breadwinner" but, in fact, most are not the sole family income contributors. The ad hoc changes in families that have two working parents and fewer children have generated social changes which are unlikely to decelerate. Thus, as individuals plan a career, they also need to plan how to use their leisure time, to develop hobbies and voluntary commitments, to rethink parenting and shared household responsibilities. At the end of the 20th century, both men and women are redefining their conceptions of adulthood; as children, they should begin to do so.

Perhaps the next question is one about financing: is 25 years sufficient to cover expenses? Certainly it is enough to cover mortgages which are usually amortized for that period. It is enough to include cars, vacations and education for the average family with 1.7 children. In Canada, social support systems are valued so much that health care is rated as the major reason for being Canadian. Other programs, including unemployment insurance, social security and child benefits ease burdens and reduce inequities. Currently, the offerings are a mumbo jumbo mix that needs to be simplified and sorted out to reduce overlaps, wastages and gaps. There are many critics but no one suggests these benefits be removed. The overall contribution to the quality of life in society is too beneficial and the negative consequences of non-support too enormous. A less overt problem involves the many people who feel trapped in a lifestyle that is not particularly rewarding; they often are distracted from serious life cycle planning by consumerism. It's a problem that needs to be discussed more in schools because the decades between living with the parental family of origin and the home that one creates as an adult are important for personal development. For most people, the time for testing how far one can fly on one's own wings or, indeed, where one wants to go and what one wants to do is during the 20s. People who don't have that time to explore often are impelled into such a period during their 30s or 40s, sometimes causing pain for others who are abandoned as the momentum of a personal quest accelerates. This type of abrupt, and misplaced transition is costly, and the price is both personal and societal.

Regardless of whether an individual expects to work in public or private sector employment or both, 25 years is sufficient. The pace of change is not identical, given that public sector changes are less market driven and more responsive to long-term pressures. While age at entry and exit to adult labor markets may vary, 25 years is sustainable. Society is renewed by multiple changes, and recycling need not be limited to material goods. People who are at the end of a cycle with a specific employer but who still want to participate have many options. They'll bring expertise and enthusiasm as initiates elsewhere. They may not receive a gold watch but they should enjoy many appreciative handshakes for their work, leisure and volunteer contributions.

The Economics of Higher Education and Impact of Technology

The model of career development described in Chapter 4 suggests that many gifted individuals will aspire to career paths that require education beyond the baccalaureate degree. The personal and financial costs of this "investment" were alluded to. The nature of this investment was powerfully described in an article by Cavanaugh, DePasquale, Hendricks and Keiger (1998) on the rising costs of tuition at The Johns Hopkins University over a 20 year period. The current yearly tuition cost of $22 600 U.S. is a dramatic increase from the $3000 U.S. 20 years ago. The price has not peaked at Johns Hopkins or any university in North America. In the Alberta context, for example, tuition at the University of Calgary continues to rise in accordance with the maximum amounts permitted by the Ministry of Advanced Education and Career Development. Several factors will assure that the costs of higher education will continue to rise in the new millennium. The major operating cost of a university is personnel cost. Through contract negotiations and merit assessments, salaries increase over time. The extensive use of the Internet requires huge investments in infrastructure costs such as cabling and computer hardware and software purchases and upgrades. Increasing regulations by governing bodies and granting agencies increase operational costs. The new Freedom of Information and Protection of Privacy Act will involve staff time, possible additional personnel and likely increased legal consultation fees. The new Ethical Guidelines developed by the major granting agencies will also involve major costs in ensuring compliance with the regulations. As the student population becomes more diverse, the need for additional resources and support systems also increases. Canadian universities are especially affected by the shrinking Canadian dollar, which makes purchases of library materials such as books and journals from the United States particularly expensive.

The main message for coping with this economic reality is the need for advanced planning. The savings and investment commitments will need to be substantially longer than in the past. Even with significant savings, students' rates of indebtedness will likely reach their highest levels in the next millennium. The rising costs will be especially difficult for individuals with limited family income. Universities will need to more effectively raise bursary funds earmarked for meritorious but needy students. Government initiatives that provide scholarship funding in exchange for future work commitments in areas of high need such as the teaching of mathematics would be helpful.

The career development transition will also be affected in the millennium by the ever-expanding role of technology in our daily lives. Computer expertise is becoming an increasing necessity in many professions. A university professor, for example, must routinely use word processing to produce potential publications, e-mail to communicate with colleagues and Internet browsers such as Netscape to gather information. There is pressure to reconfigure traditional courses for distance education delivery on the world wide web. Such reconfiguration will mean experience with presentation programs, scanning programs, audio-delivery programs and video-delivery programs.

The accessibility of computerized services will change the nature of some occupations. Most major airlines have websites that list flight itineraries, fares, and special discounts and promotions. There are also Internet travel sites that show the best fares to various destinations and provide the facility for on-line reservations. In the face of such competition, the travel agency industry will need to communicate the benefits that travel agents provide over websites. As another example, there are numerous websites offering free IQ tests. Fees for psychological assessments by chartered psychologists typically range from $400-$800. In the future, psychologists may find it difficult to compete with websites for providing some psychological services. The nature of consulting regardless of area should be greatly impacted by technology.

The success of computer entrepreneurs such as Bill Gates of Microsoft challenges some of the notions of career development presented in Chapter 4 and the milestone transitions described in Chapter 5. These models focus on educational attainment as a vehicle for career success. Bill Gates dropped out of Harvard. The developers of the Internet browser, Netscape, dropped out of Stanford. Such success stories might tempt bright and motivated individuals to pursue similar career paths. Although such successes appear to be exceptions rather than the rule, they present challenges for those counselling gifted and talented youngsters about the benefits of higher education in providing possible career paths congruent with their interests and abilities.

Preparing for Change: Whose Responsibility Is It?

It is now commonplace for people to talk about the stress that they are experiencing in attempting to keep up with the demands of change. While change can be motivating, providing the impetus for learning needed to adapt to new demands, the current pace of change and resulting impact on people has not yet fully been realized. The danger is that working and living under conditions perceived by people to be very stressful becomes a normal expectation, without considering the long-term effects for psychological and physical health. Changes in the workplace that bring demands for longer work hours and working at an intense pace challenge employees to preserve time and energy for self-care, family relationships and leisure pursuits. As we enter the 21st century, people will undoubtedly be required to adapt to the synergistic forces of change, and their capacity to adapt will be continually tested.

One of the hazards associated with the pace of change in the workplace is that change becomes a "constant state" versus "strategic change." In the first case, change becomes an ongoing condition of an organization with little direction or efforts to consolidate and evaluate the effects of change. Employees scramble to keep up with the latest directive or program without having a clear sense of how this direction is related to overall organizational goals. The image described by many employees is one of working on a treadmill in which there is no end in sight except for more hard work and few intrinsic rewards associated with working for the organization. Employees feel little commitment to organizations that function with "change for the sake of change" and ultimately perform at lower levels of productivity, decreased morale or end up leaving the organization. Part of the difficulty associated with organizations in which change is a "constant state" is an accompanying expectation that individuals assume full responsibility for managing and responding to demands of change. The rhetoric given to employees is that jobs will be made available if they are able to demonstrate their viability and contributions to the shifting goals of their organizations. Often, veiled threats are contained in working relationships that treat workers as disposable. The prerogative in such organizations is "Change!" without providing employees with assistance to adapt positively to current demands. A critical issue arises concerning the limits of people's capacity to absorb change without providing essential training for new ways of working. Rather than viewing employees as "faulty" or "incompetent" for failing to navigate demands for change, organizations need to consider their responsibility in providing leadership for working in meaningful ways.

In contrast, organizations that use "strategic change" keep clear sight of the goals for change, articulate a clear communication strategy to employees, and provide training to employees to develop effective specialist skills and general skills for managing change. Rather than assuming change as entirely the responsibility of individuals, organizations must also take responsibility for developing systemic structures to support employees to effectively manage. However, organizational career development requires commitment on the part of management to ensure successful implementation. Internal programs require allocation of resources for staff training and development programs. Organizations must be clear on the value of career development programs in the overall contribution to bottom-line goals such as productivity and profitability. Unless the viability of organizational career development can be proven as a core service to support organizational goals, it will remain at the periphery and dispensable as a "soft service" during economic fluctuations.

As we turn a page in the passage of time, the sense of awe about accomplishments in the workplace such as technological advancements and the global marketplace need to be viewed in perspective with the impact on individual and social functioning to manage change. The only certainty about the future is more change. People have to shift their perspective from considering change as an exception to be overcome to a perspective that defines life as personal transition. It is essential that people have the information, skills and resources to move with the ever-shifting flow of life. The new millenium brings images of a new start, the beginning of a new approach. Yet, that sense of optimism must be tempered with a sense of realism about people's capacities. Changing life circumstances demand that people be assisted to develop a repertoire or coping skills for managing the accompanying personal transitions. People who have the resources, both personal and economic, are likely to move forward into the new century with ease. Others will be inadequately equipped to manage the rapid pace of change and resulting demands for personal adaptation. Without deliberate efforts to prepare for future transitions, many people will simply be swept forward to face the challenges of the new millenium, ready or not.

References

Cavanaugh, J. P., DePasquale, S., Hendricks, M. & Keiger, D. (1998, September). Scrambling for dollars. *Johns Hopkins Magazine*, pp. 12-27.

Conference Board of Canada. (1992). *Employability Skills Profile: What are employers looking for?* Ottawa, ON: The Conference Board of Canada.

Day, B., Redekopp, D. & Robb, M. (1994). *Engage*. Edmonton, AB: Centre for Career Development Innovation, Concordia University College.

Elkind, D. (1988). *The hurried child : Growing up too fast too soon* (rev. ed.). Reading, MA: Addison-Wesley.

Redekopp, D. E., Day, B. & Robb, M. (1995). The "High Five" of career development. In B. Hiebert (Ed.). *Exemplary career development programs and practices: The best from Canada*. Greensboro, NC: ERIC/CASS.

A

Aboriginal people (see *Native*)
Academic demands: 49, 75, 83, 148
Academic preparation: 48, 110
Acculturation: 37-42, 47, 51, 55
Action: 64-5, 67, 72, 88
Active agent: 67, 72, 75, 88
Adaptation: 36-7, 39, 44, 46, 52
Adjustment: 40, 44-5, 47-9
Adolescent needs: 24-6, 28, 75, 87, 172
Adolescent storm and stress: 28, 172
Apprenticeship: 108, 117, 132
Assimilation: 38, 42

B

Barriers: 70, 88, 97, 126, 133
Behavioral stress control: 79, 82-3, 152
Boomerang children: 23
Bottleneck transition pattern: 107, 117

C

Career (as investment, lifestyle, mobility, possibilities, innovation): 49, 121-6, 130, 133, 142, 150, 170-1
Career (education, requirements, resources, self-efficacy, transitions): vii, xi, 14, 18-20, 76, 127, 130-3, 150, 166, 177
Career/life planning: 18-9, 21-2, 26
Change process: ix, 63-7
Charting progress: 68-9, 73
Cognitive stress control: 79, 82, 152
Commitment: 68-9
Communication skills: 53, 81, 95-6, 103, 108-11, 128, 141, 147
Conference Board of Canada: 76-7, 96-9, 105, 110, 112-13, 172
Conflict resolution: 54, 81
Contemplation: 64, 88
Contract: 69, 73, 142, 156, 158, 176
Coping (repertoires, skills, strategies): 24, 27-8, 37, 51-5, 70, 77-8, 82, 88, 130, 143, 148, 151-2, 159-60, 169, 177, 179
Counsellor(s): 35, 77, 107, 114, 129, 132, 159, 162
Creative problem-solving: 128, 133, 142
Critical incidents: 55
Cross-cultural (competencies, friendships, training, transitions): xi, 35-41, 44-55, 159-62, 170
Cultural (conflict, diversity, knowledge, self-awareness, skills, taxonomies): vi, xi, 23, 25, 29, 35, 43-4, 46-7, 49, 52-3, 95, 123, 160, 162, 170
Culture shock: 36-7, 51

D

Demographic changes: 14-5, 18, 35, 56, 93, 117, 174
Discrimination: 44, 49, 126-7, 156
Dominant and non-dominant groups: 38-42, 51-2
Drudgery: 19-21

E

Easy passage transition pattern: 108, 116-17, 157
Education: 41-2, 44-5, 49-50, 93-6 101-2, 105-8, 112-13, 116-17, 123, 129, 132, 138-9, 169-71, 174-7
Educational and guidance personnel: 131
Educational transitions: 150

Employability Skills Profile: 76, 81, 96-7, 108-11, 118, 172

Employees: 46-7, 95-6, 98-9, 102, 105, 110, 113-14, 118, 170, 174, 178-9

Employers: 35, 46, 93, 95-9, 102, 104-6, 108, 110, 112-16, 118, 167, 176

Employment: 38, 41-2, 44-5, 49-50, 54-5, 81, 93-5, 98-101, 103-6, 108-9, 111-12, 114-17, 133, 156, 158-61, 166, 169, 171, 174-5

Empowerment: vii, 88

Ethnocentrism: 51

Evaluating progress: 68, 147

Exam writing: 80-1, 84-5, 108, 111, 140-1

Exercise: 78, 86

Expectations: 17, 38, 48, 72, 114, 123, 125-27, 147-9

F

Family conflict: 40, 45

Floundering transition pattern: 107-8, 117, 157

Friends: 95, 100, 108, 117, 157, 160-1, 164, 166-7

G

Gender roles: 49, 111,

Global economy: 35, 96, 169-71

Globalization: vi, 13-4, 18

Goal setting: 67, 69, 73, 87, 110

H

High 5: 21-2, 76, 173

Homosexual youth: 28

I

Immigrants: 16, 35, 41, 43-5, 49, 158, 162

Integration: 38, 45

Intergenerational conflict: 40, 42

International students: xi, 23, 35, 41, 48-50

International work: 46

Interpersonal skills: 37, 53, 75, 108, 111, 128-9, 133, 142-5, 172

Intrapersonal skills: 37, 53, 108, 111

J

Job entry: 102, 108-12, 117, 158

L

Labor market: 15-6, 76, 94, 99-100, 104, 109, 114-15, 117-18, 158, 174, 176

Language proficiency: 39-40, 44-5, 48-9, 159

Learning: 19, 21-2, 35-8, 40, 45, 50, 52, 56, 71, 76, 82, 96, 105-6, 108, 110, 112, 114-15, 118, 132, 143, 147, 159-60, 170, 178

Life skills: 70

Lifestyle: 39-40, 42, 44, 63, 85-6, 95, 100-1, 114, 122-3, 125, 133, 175

Linkage programs: 103

M

Maintenance: 64-7

Marginalization: 38

Matches: vi, 93, 95-6, 99, 105-6, 108, 111-16, 118

Megatrend(s): 93, 112, 117

Miniature adult syndrome: 86

Mismatches (see *Matches*)

Motivation: 71

N

NAFTA: 14

Native (First Nations, Indian, etc.): 17, 23, 28, 35, 41-3, 101, 104, 106
Northwest Territories: 17, 41
Note taking: 83-4, 140
Nutrition: 78, 85-6

O

Ongoing personal and social problems transition pattern: 106, 117
Oppression: 41-2

P

Parents: 13, 17-8, 23-5, 75, 77, 81, 86-7, 97, 99, 101, 103, 106, 112, 114-15, 122-3, 126, 131, 137, 146-51, 163, 166, 173, 175
Part-time work: 15, 26, 76, 97-101, 103-4, 109, 111, 113-15, 118, 140, 158, 167, 174
Passing through transition pattern: 106, 117
Peer(s): 75, 95, 114, 126, 131, 140, 148
Perception: 75, 77, 87, 93, 95-7, 99, 102, 105, 112, 126, 130-1, 144, 171-2, 175
Personal agency: 67, 72, 75
Personal management: 76, 97, 110-11, 172
Personal vision: 70, 88, 173
Physiological stress control: 79, 82
Post-migration stage: 44-5
Pre-migration stage: 44-5
Precontemplation: 64, 69
Predeparture programs: 46, 52
Preparation stage: 64-6
Problem-solving: 47, 53, 55, 75-6, 83, 110, 141
Psychological adaptation: 37

Q

Quieting Reflex (QR): 82, 85

R

Racism: 44-5, 49, 51, 127
Re-entry transition pattern: 38-9, 108
Refugees: 35, 41, 43
Relationship transitions: 18, 23, 144-5, 151
Relaxation: 82
Reservations: 42
Residential school experience: 42-3
Resumé: 109, 111, 132-3
Role changes: 39

S

School leavers: 15, 17, 98-9, 100, 104, 112, 118, 138
Self-awareness: 50-1, 54, 142
Self-concept: 38, 71, 87, 130-1, 142
Self-efficacy: 72
Self-esteem: 25, 71-6, 82, 110, 146, 167, 172, 174
Self-management: 67, 69, 73, 110-11
Self-talk: 72-4, 85
Separation: 23, 38
Sex-role stereotyping: 129
Skill sets: vi, x, 18, 29, 63, 77, 86, 88, 93, 95, 108-9, 111, 115-16, 173
Sleep: 78
Social isolation: 39, 48
Social skills: 23
Social support: 23-4, 47, 55, 78-9, 159, 161, 171, 175
Social transition: 49
Socialization: 27, 38, 42, 51, 123, 126, 175
SQ3R: 84

Stress: 24-8, 37-8, 41, 45, 47-8, 54-5, 72-3, 77-83, 85-7, 100, 130, 137, 151, 158-9, 172, 178
Stress management: 54-5, 79, 82, 85-6, 130, 133, 140-3
Stressor management: 79
Students: v, x, 24, 48, 87, 93-4, 97-104, 106, 108, 110, 112-18, 122, 128, 140-1, 143, 148-9, 162-5, 167, 170-1, 176-7
Students, with disabilities: xi, 74

Workplace behavior: 46

T

Teamwork: 76, 97, 103, 106, 110-11, 172
Technology: 14, 18, 93-4, 98, 100, 102, 110, 124, 126, 169, 171, 176-7, 179
Thinking – critical and creative: 76, 96, 108-10, 114, 172
Time management: 81, 84, 100, 108, 110-11, 130, 133, 140-3
Transition process: v, 28, 36, 63, 94-5, 97, 99, 105-6, 114, 116, 139, 161
Trauma: 44-5

U

Unemployment: 15, 81, 94, 99-102, 138, 175
Unskilled jobs: 16

V

Values conflict: 38
Vision: 70-1
Voluntary migration: 44

W

Work: 17-20, 27, 35, 38-9, 47, 55
Work force: 14, 16, 96, 138, 170
Work teams: 47, 55
Workload: 26-7